DUNCAN GRANT

and the Bloomsbury Group

"Two Nude Figures, Embracing." (collection of the author: DBT.56)

DUNCAN GRANT

and the Bloomsbury Group

by Douglas Blair Turnbaugh

A Mario Sartori Book

Lyle Stuart Inc.   *Secaucus, New Jersey*

Published by Lyle Stuart Inc.
120 Enterprise Ave., Secaucus, N.J. 07094
In Canada; Musson Book Company
A division of General Publishing Co. Limited.
Don Mills, Ontario

Queries regarding rights and permissions should be
addressed to: Lyle Stuart, 120 Enterprise Avenue,
Secaucus, N.J. 07094

Library of Congress Cataloging-in-Publication Data

Turnbaugh, Douglas Blair
    Duncan Grant and the Bloomsbury Group.

    "A Mario Sartori book."
    Bibliography: p.
    Includes index.
    1. Grant, Duncan, 1885-1978. 2. Painters--England--
Biography. 3. Painting, English. 4. Painting, Modern--
20th century--England. 5. Bloomsbury group. I. Title.
II. Title: Duncan Grant.
ND497.G68T87   1987   759.2 [B]   87-17998
ISBN 0-8184-0442-6

Manufactured in the United States of America.

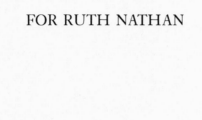

FOR RUTH NATHAN

Acknowledgments

The author gratefully thanks the following people for help of various kinds during the writing of this book:

Peter Alexander, Lord Annan, Nick Ashley, Dominick Attanasio, Rob Baker, Julian Barran, Mary-Claire Barton, Peter Berliant, Patricia Boutelle, Sarah Bradley, staff at British Information Services (New York City), Chris Brown, David Burnett, Frances Chaves, the Rt. Hon. Alan Clark, Louise Crawford, Richard Crosland, Peter Day, Jean-Luc Degonde, Barbara Della Bianca, the Duchess of Devonshire, the Duke of Devonshire, the Marchioness of Dufferin and Ava, Edwin Fancher, John Ferrone, Donatella Geddes, Hugh Geddes, Lindsay Geddes, Jeffrey Gerecke, Anita Gilodo, the Rev. Davis Given, the late Duncan Grant, Lee Grunden, Frances Guest, Irwin Haims, Carolyn Heilbrun, John Herman, HRH the Princess of Hesse and the Rhine, Stuart Hodes, Kenneth Hood, Damaris Horan, Dr. Lenard Jacobson, Marion Kirley, Richard Kostelanetz, Aldon James, Katherine Law, Linda Lawson, Dr. and Mrs. Nicholas Macris, Bill McBrien, Malcolm Cormack, Joseph McCrindle, D. J. McDonald, Robert Miller, Nicoletta Misch, Richard Morphet, Paul Nathan, Ruth Nathan, Patrick O'Connor, Mary Louise Gallaway Okajima, Louise Page, Kevin Patterson, Tim and Sharon Patterson, Richard Perkins, Leslie Pockell, Richard Prince, Bill Pritchet, James Purdy, Katherine Sharp Rachlis, Martha Rafferty, Perry Rathbone, Pat Gilbert Read, Chris Reed, Duncan Robinson, Clarissa Roche, Cordelia Roche, Paul Roche, Tobit Roche, Countess Emilie Rohan-Chandor, Stephanie Rose, the late Jane Sabersky, Mario Sartori, Randy Schmit, Elizabeth Schub, Jenny Schulman, Douglas Schwegler, Richard Shone, Hayuta Skayan, Lowery Stokes Sims, Pandora Smith, Diana Stammers, Tung Ai Tam, Peter Tcherepnine, Decherd Turner, Juliet Walker, Thomas Wheeler, the Dowager Countess Wimborne, Elizabeth Winn, Jack Woody

The author and publishers wish to thank the following for permission to reproduce work from their collections:

Her Majesty Queen Elizabeth the Queen Mother
Her Grace the Duchess of Devonshire
His Grace the Duke of Devonshire
The Marchioness of Dufferin and Ava
Thos. Agnew & Sons, London
Durban Art Museum, South Africa
Fitzwilliam Museum, Cambridge
Carolyn Heilbrun
King's College, Cambridge
Metropolitan Museum of Art, New York
National Gallery of Victoria, Melbourne
National Portrait Gallery, London
New York Public Library, Dance Collection
Kevin Patterson
The Reader's Digest Association, Inc.
Cordelia Roche
Paul Roche
Tobit Roche
Mario Sartori
David Shapiro
Pandora Smith
The Tate Archive, London
The Tate Gallery, London
Harry Ransom Humanities Research Center, University of Texas at Austin
The Toledo Museum of Art
Victoria and Albert Museum, London
Elizabeth Winn
Yale Center for British Art, New Haven

Preface

MY FIRST EXPOSURE to the work of Duncan Grant was a black and white reproduction of "The Bathers" (see Number 88) in Germain Bazin's *Modern Painting*, 1951. Eager to see more of his work, I was surprised and frustrated to find him almost entirely forgotten or unknown. It was then an unexpected delight and pleasure to discover him alive and well, still as enchanting as could be, and to be able to know him, however briefly. The late Jane Sabersky, Curator of Art Properties at Columbia University, was the first to encourage me to try to publish his drawings. This book could not have been written without the generous cooperation of Paul Roche, a long-time friend and a principal heir of Duncan Grant. Mr. Roche answered all my questions with patience and candor, gave me unlimited access to his collection and to all his Grant material, as well as his own records and unpublished journals. I am also grateful to the Duchess of Devonshire for her interest and helpful suggestions, and to the Duke of Devonshire for contributing the Foreword to this book. Special thanks to Chris Reed. It is through Ruth Nathan's untiring efforts and Mario Sartori's confidence in the proposal that this book was finally realized.

Contents

Duncan Grant

A Memory

by the Duke of Devonshire

MY WIFE AND I did not meet Duncan Grant until the 1950's. By then he was an old man in years but not in spirit. He retained all the charm and much of the looks of his youth and it was very easy to understand why so many people, men and women, had loved him.

A mutual friend, Mrs. Violet Hammersley, brought him into our lives. Her sharp, though never waspish, tongue was a perfect foil to his gentle, tolerant attitude to the world and its problems and together they made the best company imaginable.

At Chatsworth there is a portrait of Duncan as a young man, painted by Vanessa Bell. It shows him in all his golden youth. In old age the gold was untarnished but of a deeper hue. There was still the thick hair, the sweep of the jaw and above all the sooty-fingered upturned eyes which seemed always on the verge of smiling.

More striking even than his looks was his charm: a quality impossible to describe in words or in paint. It has to be witnessed. So will Duncan be remembered, gentle, charming and handsome, always a delightful companion.

We are both glad there are some of his paintings at Chatsworth. They reflect his character, giving warmth to the rooms in which they hang. They portray a world distant from that we live in now, one in which the pace was slower, manners were better, a place more civilized to live in.

Andrew Devonshire
Lismore Castle
16 April 1987

PART I

1885–1946

A Historical Outline

Family connections are part of the poetry of history—LORD ANNAN

CHAPTER 1

1885–1905

DUNCAN JAMES CORROWR GRANT was born on January 21, 1885, in the Scottish highlands, at The Doune, the Grants' family house, at Rothiemurchus, in Inverness-shire. He was the only child of Major Bartle Grant (1860-1924) and Ethel McNeil Grant (1863-1948). They had returned on leave from India, where Major Grant was on duty with his regiment, so that their child could be born in the family home. Ethel has been described as a penniless Scottish girl of great beauty. Bartle was one of eight children on a branch of the enormous and ancient family tree of the Grants, a family prominent in the history of Scotland, and in the British Empire at the height of its glory.

Duncan was descended from John Grant, 4th laird of Freuchie, Chief of Grant, an eminent figure in the time of Queen Elizabeth I. John Grant married Lady Marjorie Stuart in 1539, thereby making Duncan a potential claimant to the Scottish throne. They had two sons, Duncan (d. 1582), through whom descend the Chiefs of Grant, and Patrick (d. 1617) from whom the Grants of Rothiemurchus are descended.

Duncan's grandfather was Sir John Peter Grant, GCMG, KCB, (1807-93) who served as a governor in India and later as Governor of Jamaica. The Doune had long been in the possession of his family. It was located in Rothiemurchus, a tiny and remote village hidden away in the Grampian mountains and isolated from all neighbors by the fast flowing River Spey. The Rothiemurchus Forest still today has one of the few remaining stretches of natural Scotch pine, and the estate realized considerable income from sale of its timber, which was logged and floated down the Spey. Salmon from the river are still appreciated by gourmets all over the world. The house was plain and comfortless until the 1870's, when Sir John enlarged and modernized it, adding outbuildings for the army of servants necessary to maintain the establishment.

The Doune was then used almost as a resort hotel by hordes of relatives and friends. Patrick Grant, a cousin of Duncan's, wrote: "During the summer months the house was packed, often with the whole Strachey family, my first cousins." Although The Doune must have been crowded, it was a happy place. Children could play on the grass, eat ripe strawberries fresh from the garden and ride ponies. There were plays and charades. Reading aloud from the classics, including of course Sir Walter Scott, was a pastime. There were sketching, painting and literary efforts at all levels.

Patrick Grant wrote that while at The Doune "Lytton Strachey and I decided we must produce and edit a magazine...it represents, I think, Lytton's very first attempts at creative writing. Little did we guess that in the days to come he could become a famous author. His sister Pernel...was kind enough to write it out for us, and everyone, even including the butler, wrote stories or verses for it. Lytton's father, old Sir Richard, even painted a picture for us, but though it was a great success there was never a sequel to the first number."

Those who might long for respite from these intellectual activities could walk in the primeval forests, wade in streams, and climb the slopes of the near-by Cairngorm mountains. Years later, Lytton remembered the natural beauty of the place, "its massive and imposing landscape, its gorgeous colouring, its hidden places of solitude and silence, its luxuriant vegetation, its wilderness of remote and awful splendor." Duncan shared with his cousin a love of the place, and its dramatic landscape made deep impressions on his visual memories.

Duncan remembered his grandparents at The Doune. He told Paul Roche:[1] "I'd see him being wheeled about in a bath chair—quite stricken down. I don't think you could talk to him. He had a man servant who looked after him. My grandmother lived in a wing of her own.... He just nodded to people he knew. He never spoke—not to me, anyhow." Paul joked in reply: "He probably thought you stemmed from Lord Raglan." "I dare say," Duncan responded. This referred to the indiscretions of Lady Grant, Duncan's grandmother, Henrietta Chichele. Duncan remembered his grandmother as

---

[1]See *With Duncan Grant In Southern Turkey*, by Paul Roche.

"of an earlier age, not Victorian at all. She had the morals of a Regency period." He told that while in India, Lady Grant had gone to one of the hill stations—Juggerata or perhaps Musoorie—during the hot weather and while Sir John was off "being Governor of Madras or perhaps Bengal" she enjoyed a liaison with Lord Raglan or "I'm not so sure it wasn't Cardigan."

Sir John returned from the plains to find his wife with child. He forgave her. "The result was Aunt Hennie. What's so extraordinary is that the whole thing happened again the year after." Sir John returned to find her with child again, by the same lover. The result was Uncle George. Aunt Hennie and Uncle George were brought up with the rest of the family. Aunt Hennie, according to Duncan, "was dropped on her head as a child. Yes, from a cab in Rome. They were driving and she was thrown out on her head. She behaved oddly for the rest of her life....She used to be sent out for long walks. Sometimes I went with her. We got on very well together. She and I were on the same intellectual level." Aunt Hennie was the only one of Lady Grant's children not to marry.

Lady Grant led a *vita activa*. While travelling back and forth around the world, she produced eight children. One of them, Jane Maria, was born at sea on board the East India Company's *The Earl of Hardcastle*, during a ferocious storm off the Cape of Good Hope, in 1840. As well as Bartle, Jane, Hennie and George, the other four children were: the eldest, John Peter Grant, who became laird of Rothiemurchus (succeeding his father John Peter Grant, and succeeded by his son, John Peter Grant); Frances Elinor, who married Sir James Colvile, and became a smart hostess at her elegant house in Park Lane; Charles, who became a captain in the Black Watch, stationed variously in Gibralter and Egypt; and Trevor.

Uncle George (one of Lady Grant's indiscretions) became a distinguished Indian civil servant. As a child, Duncan had spent time in his house at Winchester, but "never took to him." Duncan recalled George was the only brother who wasn't musical.

Charles and George both had sons named Pat. To ease the confusion, and with certain moral implications, one was called "White Pat" and the other "Black Pat." One of them eventually ran off with the other's wife. Many activities in this busy family which might have been considered scandalous by proper Victorians seem to have been accepted without great fuss. Charles' marriage to a Jewess, Agnes Isaacs, created a certain stir in the family, but as exotica could not compare with Uncle Trevor's marriage to a "dusky native" of India, Clementina Gouldsbury, a half-caste lady said to have made chupatties on the drawing room carpet. Uncle Trevor and Aunt Clementina's numerous sons "stayed mostly in India." Duncan remembers that Uncle Trevor "kept a huge enlarged photograph [of Clementina] on an easel in his sitting room. He read practically all night and Mrs. Masters his housekeeper gave him a sort of breakfast-lunch at about twelve or one. When he was not reading he used to play the cello for hours together. I thought him very flirtatious with his Strachey nieces, and I remember him with his hand nearly always around Pippa's waist." Uncle Trevor was killed by a bear.

Duncan's father and mother, Bartle Grant and Ethel McNeil, made an attractive couple. In photographs taken about the time of their marriage, in their early twenties, each is remarkably beautiful. Ethel had a sensual, rather androgynous face. She could have modelled for the Pre-Raphaelites. Bartle, in his elaborately frogged and sashed officer's uniform, is a model of youthful confidence, intelligence and virility. He was not oblivious to the effect he had on ladies. Bartle had many affairs. According to Duncan, his mother never showed any signs of resenting these escapades. But then, in the best tradition of the family, Ethel flirted outrageously and had a lover of her own.

As with many younger sons of prominent families, a military career had been assigned to Bartle as well as his brother Charles. Bartle was originally with the 8th Hussars, later joining another regiment, and was manager of the Royal Artillery Mess at Woolwich. Although professionally involved with the practical side of his army responsibilities, he most certainly did not let it dominate his life. He was well educated and an avid reader in many subjects. He was a botanist and wrote *The Orchids of Burma*. He was known as a cook, and was a first-rate musician. He composed drawing room songs, and was conducting the orchestra of a travelling company of musical comedy when the South African War broke out and he had to join his regiment in Malta. Duncan said his father was too educated and too civilized for the army. "Music was his passion. He and his brothers were friends of Joachim and his quartet, especially Piatti the cellist, who once took me on his knee at the age of four and promised to make a good cellist of me...." Bartle and his brothers and sisters could argue by the hour about music.

Besides music, Bartle loved pretty women. At least one of his affairs was more than a mere escapade. The lady was named Polly. Duncan: "...One of his affairs, I think was much more serious, with probably a child. He took me once to the opera with this old love of his and her son, who was just my age. And I always wondered if he was my father's son.... We went to see *HMS Pinafore* and both loved it.... I remember Aunt Violet [his mother Ethel's sister] laughing with my father over a photograph of Polly as if it were a known thing, their affair."

Paul Roche asked Duncan if he thought it sad that such a beautiful pair as Bartle and Ethel should so soon have fallen out of love. "Yes," Duncan answered, "but I don't think they were ever sad about it. With my father, affairs were inevitable and my mother accepted the fact. No one thought ill of her for going her own way too." By the time Duncan was about sixteen, Ethel's affair with a Commander Young "was already a going thing." Duncan thought it was his father who had to accept the situation. "I think she was quite happy with that [her relationship with Commander Young], a much more important event in her life than my father's [affairs] . . . Because it was a real love affair." After Bartle was posted to Malta, Ethel made a hit with the officers there. She conducted a flirtation with the Commander-in-Chief, Admiral Fisher, who insisted on dancing with her every evening.

Duncan's early childhood was spent with his parents in India and Burma, returning to Britain with them every two years for home leave, until 1894. He was educated during this period by his governess Alice Bates. He loved to draw and incorporated into his boyish fantasies elements observed in India (Numbers 29 and 30). When he was nine, he was sent home alone to England to attend school. "My grannie [Lady Grant] was at Southampton to meet me. . . . She had a lovely old house in Chiswick, Hogarth House. I lived with her and found her delightful. Everything she said interested me."

From 1894-99, he attended Hillbrow Preparatory School, Rugby (Number 1), where his fellow students included his cousin and best friend James Strachey and Rupert Brooke. Settling in at Hillbrow, he was a great success with his classmates, thanks to his tales of India, until "some nasty little brat—jealous no doubt—started the idea that 'Grant goes on and on about India' and they all turned on me." Duncan quickly discovered that "one was left alone if good at games. So I made up my mind to be good at football." And he was.

A memorable event of his days at Hillbrow was the scandal caused by the disgrace of Mr. Eden, the headmaster. Mr. Eden liked to whip his boys with the birch. He would hum before doing it. Duncan recalled that "Whenever we heard humming down the passage we all knew what it meant—a birching somewhere." He whipped Duncan occasionally "with pleasure . . . Though he wasn't improper. He did his birching straightforwardly." Birching boys was an approved practice. However, Mr. Eden did like to visit "little boys while they were having their baths" and "did do . . . improper gestures towards" favorites. One of these told his father, and there was "a frightful scandal." Mr. Eden was ordered to leave the school immediately, and he fled in terror. Rupert Brooke somehow learned where he was hiding and went to get him, convincing the desperate man to come back to the school, "pack up quietly and leave in decent order." Rupert probably saved him from suicide, in Duncan's view, a remarkable act for a boy of fifteen or sixteen.

Although Duncan's parents were not religious, they made the conventional Victorian gestures. Duncan's religious instruction climaxed with a mystical experience. During his confirmation by the bishop, he saw Christ coming up the aisle. "He stopped and laid his hand on me." When Duncan told his friend James Strachey about the vision, James' way of dealing with it was to say, "Well, let's look up Christianity in the *Encyclopaedia Brittanica*," and he read it out to Duncan. "He then turned to me and said 'Do you mean to say you believe all this?' The effect was instantaneous. My Christianity fell away from me like a mantle."

In 1899, Duncan was sent to St. Paul's School in London, where he was put in the army class. He now lived with Sir Richard and Lady Strachey and their children. Although he was happy with them, in later years he described himself as "the dumped grass-orphan of an Anglo-Indian major." Lady Strachey was Jane Maria Grant, who had been born in the storm at sea. She had married Sir Richard, who had been appointed secretary to her father while he was in Calcutta during the Mutiny. They had thirteen children, three of whom died in infancy. Of their many accomplished children, the most famous was Lytton Strachey (1880-1932). This family lived packed together with butlers and servants in their notoriously ugly, seven-story Italianate mansion at 69 Lancaster Gate. This would be Duncan's home until 1906, although he still went abroad at times with his parents, and visited Malta in 1900 when his father was stationed there.

Already a sociable creature, Duncan had, as well as his cousins, an eye for new friends. On his way home from St. Paul's, he used to stop for tea with a family with four children. Of them, he says, "I fell deeply in love with Elly and Horace." His infatuation was noticed and his mother asked whether he was fond of Elly. He admitted he was fond of her, but noted, "I suppose it wasn't so obvious that I was deeply attached to Horace."

Paul Roche said that Duncan never mentioned having any sexual experiences at school, just "perhaps some fiddling," and believes this was not from lack of interest but from lack of privacy. Duncan was a day student, without the opportunities available to the boarding students for night-time adventures. He was also thereby spared the sexual assaults so frequently committed by older boys on the younger ones in public schools. This may account for Duncan's lack of interest in sadomasochism, not infrequently a shaping element in the lives of men subjected to the public school experience.

Although in India Sir Richard had been known for his forceful manner and hot temper, back in England he became a little vague and devoted himself to meteorology and other scientific interests, and to reading six novels a week, delivered by van to the house and then on to him on a silver tray. Lady Strachey was the dominant figure at 69 Lancaster Gate, and she concerned herself less with the business of housekeeping than with affairs of the mind, in talk of literature or in arranging musicales in the drawing room. It was a fertile environment for creativity. There were play writing and play acting and games of every sort. Almost all her children became accomplished writers and shared a love of music. Cousins James and Marjorie spent hours with Duncan at the piano, going through the latest Gilbert and Sullivan. It was here that Duncan learned to dance Scottish reels and the sword dance.

Duncan (Number 2) was thought to be intellectually slow (his Uncle Trevor considered him an imbecile), and expectations for his career in the Army were not promising. In drill, his rifle constantly fell to the ground and of mathematics he understood nothing whatsoever. He was switched from the army class to the chemistry class, where he did no better. "Aunt Janie, that wonderful woman, came to my rescue," Duncan remembered. Lady Strachey has earned a place in the history of art by persuading Duncan's parents to allow him to study art. She wrote to Lytton in 1901 that "The great excitement is about Duncan who appears likely to turn out to be a genius of an artist...but what to do with him is the difficulty."[2]

The difficulty was solved in 1901 by sending him to the Westminster School of Art, where he studied until 1905. (At some point he was denied admission to the Royal Academy school, one of the few setbacks in his long career, and a rejection which pained him deeply.) Duncan used to pray every day that he could learn to paint like Edward Burne-Jones. He learned more from a group of fellow students than from the teachers. In particular, Marius Forestier—who admired the French Impressionists, especially Monet and Sisley—became a good friend.

Professional guidance in Duncan's career came from the French artist Simon Bussy, who had married cousin Dorothy Strachey. Bussy impressed Duncan with his industry and his honesty. "A painter had to paint every day no matter what he felt like," Duncan remembered. He also learned the value of copying old masters, and "Simon made me see that it wasn't enough to put together the harmonious elements of a composition; one had to focus them and fuse them into a whole. 'Every picture should have in it *un clou*,' he used to say: a point which pins the whole design together."

[2]*Lytton Strachey,* by Michael Holroyd, p. 261.

A sketch book dated 1902 shows Duncan's wide range of visual interests. Every page is different, with portrait sketches, nude studies, animals, birds, landscapes, architectural notes, and classical statuary filling the pages (Numbers 32 and 33). The summer of 1902 was happily spent at Streatley-on-Thames, where his parents were staying in a house lent by Uncle Harcourt, from his mother's side of the family. His uncle would take him sketching in a punt before breakfast. Duncan made many drawings (Number 31) and paintings. "The Kitchen," 1902 (Number 34), is one of his earliest surviving paintings. Now in the Tate Gallery, this painting contains elements which would concern him throughout his life—views from one room to another, varied patterns on wallpapers and floor, the figure and the bottles, jugs and fruit of still life.

When Duncan was about seventeen, his parents decided his health required a holiday in the south of France, and he went to stay at Lady Colvile's Villa Henriette in the south of France. En route, in Paris, Duncan discovered a shop "given over to licentious literature" where he picked up a copy of *How We Lost Our Virginity*. He read this on the train journey south and then forgot about it, putting it away with his clothes. The butler later discovered the wicked book and took it to Uncle Trevor when he arrived at the villa. Uncle Trevor was horrified and took Duncan at once to a doctor in Nice who suggested madness might result from such reading. Back at the villa, Lady Colvile told him, in the most affectionate way, "I'm very sorry but I think your parents want you home."

Back in London, sensible Aunt Janie, mother of five boys, including the outrageous Lytton, said, "What nonsense! Pay no attention to it. Boys will be boys." But Major Grant took his son to see Dr. Hyslop, head of the lunatic asylum at Bedlam. Duncan felt immediately at ease, sensing that the doctor was "such a completely humane, decent sort of lively person." Dr. Hyslop turned out to be a painter, too, and reassured Major Grant, comforting him that his son was in no danger.

Duncan's notable equanimity was operating early on and he was not seriously troubled by the inanities of his uncle and the incompetent doctor in Nice. Characteristically, Duncan's confidence in his own impulses and intuitions saved him from any debilitating introspection and all his energy was free to flow into his work and friendships. He never seemed to experience any sense of guilt about his affectional preferences and so never shied away from them. In later years he told his daughter one of his favorite maxims: *never be ashamed.* She believes that he lived up to this, "having early realized that candor is the key to peace of mind." This candor is all the more remarkable in the moral climate of Victorian England.[3]

In 1903 he again spent the summer in Streatley-on-Thames, and also visited the Hebrides and Holland. Streatley-on-Thames was a place he loved all his life. It was there when he was about eighteen years old that he had his second mystical experience. He heard a voice, loud and clear, "like a command... 'You must go out into the world and learn all there is to know and be seen in the world of painting. The Impressionists you must see and learn from and there are other things going on at this very moment about which you know nothing.'"

In the winter of 1904 he and his mother went to Italy, with a party of friends which included Helen Maitland, who later married the artist Boris Anrep. They stayed in Florence, at the Bertolli hotel on the Lungarno, with Mrs. Grant's cousin Mrs. Ewebank and her three daughters in a flat nearby. Rupert Brooke appeared briefly. There were picnics and expeditions and lively conversations. Duncan also visited Siena, Rome and Arezzo, where he was greatly impressed by the frescoes of Piero della Francesca. He followed Simon Bussy's advice. In the Uffizi, he copied della Francesca's portrait of Federigo da Montefeltro, and, on commission from Harry Strachey, part of Masaccio's frescoes in the Brancacci Chapel in Santa Maria del Carmine. He also studied Giotto and Veronese.

As well as working hard at painting, Duncan refined the art of meeting new friends. He told Paul Roche about an elegant young German he had met as they both stood gazing into the Arno. The German was also copying in the Uffizi and was obviously rich, because he had a servant to carry his paint box. He took Duncan driving in an open carriage, the fashionable thing to do at four in the afternoon, round the Cascine Gardens. One day he asked Duncan: "Are you 'homme-femme' or 'femme-homme'?" Duncan said he found that difficult to answer. He knew the reference to Plato's man-woman... but "what on earth did he mean by "femme-homme?"

---

[3]The infamous Labouchere Amendment in 1885 made sex acts between men (but not between women) a crime subject to imprisonment at hard labor. This was the law of the land during most of Duncan's lifetime. It had been used to ruin Oscar Wilde in 1895, an event which frightened many men into new circumspection, and which served to enforce a censorship on the work of many creative artists. It was in force until July 27, 1967, when the Homosexual Bill became law. This statute made sex in private between two consenting male adults no longer a legal offense and fixed the age of adulthood at twenty-one.

CHAPTER 2

Bloomsbury

As a YOUTH, Duncan lived with the Stracheys during the time when Lytton was at university. In 1905, Lytton, twenty-five years old, finally left Cambridge and came home to his parents' house in London. He fell passionately in love with his twenty-year-old cousin, who had just left the Westminster School of Art. Their relationship propelled Duncan into the group of friends, most slightly older than he, that were to be known as "Bloomsbury." Almost all of these remarkable men and women achieved fame in their various careers, and for their long-enduring friendships. Here is a brief introduction to the major figures Duncan was to encounter:

LYTTON STRACHEY: Lady Strachey was 40 and Sir Richard was 63, and had been retired for ten years, when Lytton, their eleventh child, was born (with two more to come). When Lytton was a little boy, Lady Strachey (like Lady Wilde, Oscar's mother) dressed her long-haired son in skirts, because he looked prettier that way. He was a frail child, dependent on his mother, and his life-long insecurity may be related to the birth of his brother James, seven years his junior. From the age of three, his literature-loving mother read to him not only her own verses but Shakespeare and Elizabethan drama as well. She held him on her knee while she played the piano, and enjoyed parlor games with him. Later, a misfit at school, he was the object of much bullying.

Lytton hoped to go to Oxford but was rejected. He went instead to Cambridge University. There, at Trinity College, some of his rich, hearty classmates "wished to throw him into the fountain in the Great Court to demonstrate their dissatisfaction with him, but on the whole he was allowed to occupy this place quietly as a harmless mutant, regarded more with curiosity than distaste."[1] However, his intelligence and outrageous wit were appreciated by a group of bright young men which included Thoby Stephen, Leonard

---

[1] *The Loving Friends,* by David Gadd, p. 12.

Woolf, Clive Bell, and Maynard Keynes (who was to become one of the most important economists of the twentieth century).

Lytton joined several undergraduate groups, but the most important for him was the exclusive Cambridge Conversazione Society. As its membership was limited to twelve, it was also known as the Apostles. It was a secret society and differed from other university organizations in that its members did not cease to belong once they had graduated from Cambridge. They met behind locked doors to read and discuss papers. "Essentially it was a secret brotherhood of the elect who sought truth and self-development through absolute candor with each other. A prime article of the Apostle's faith was unworldliness and the pursuit of truth or the promotion of a good cause, regardless of what ordinary mortals might think."[2]

There were categories of membership in the brotherhood, from "embryos" (those being considered for election) to the "angels" (those who had left the university). Lytton was elated by his election to the Society, in 1902 (he noted that he was the Society's 239th member), and his intellectual and social life began to bloom. For one thing, there were members from all the colleges of the university, particularly King's, Maynard's college, and for another, many of the older brethren still attended meetings (although they could not vote). Lytton was able to become acquainted with Desmond MacCarthy, Bertrand Russell, George Edward Moore, and other distinguished minds.

Moore, a moral philosopher, had just published his influential *Principia Ethica*. For Lytton, Moore became "the prophet of that divine companionship for which he so urgently yearned." Moore's "emphasis on friendship, at a time when there was so little understanding of sexual deviance, meant to him 'the glorification of that friendship which, throughout the Victorian Age of Unreason, had dared not speak its name.'"[3] With Moore as his prophet, Lytton was sexually liberated and eventually was also able to pursue his creative life.

JOHN MAYNARD KEYNES: Maynard had parents of remarkable distinction (as was usual with this group of people), with a family tree heavy with fascinating ancestors, dating back to 1066. His father, John Neville Keynes, was the chief administrative officer of Cambridge University and his mother, Florence Ada, was Cambridge's first woman councillor and later its mayor. The Keyneses had three children and lavished love and attention on them, but Maynard, the eldest, was their pet.

---

[2] *John Maynard Keynes,* by Charles Hession, p. 43.

[3] *John Maynard Keynes,* by Charles Hession, p. 45-6.

His intellect developed rapidly, and his wide range of interests was noted early on. As a student he developed a habit of staying late in bed and working there, a habit which continued all his life. Special tutors were hired to help him win a scholarship to Eton. At Eton, he was very competitive and began to flourish. His tutor wrote to his parents that Maynard had "a real healthy interest in all the doings of the college, athletic and otherwise" and "Maynard will be returning to you with honors thick upon him."

English public schools are worlds unto themselves, and have been described as the most sexual places in the world and the public school experience was overwhelmingly one of erotic and romantic passion. Maynard chose as friends at Eton notably handsome boys, with homosexual sensibilities, including Bernard Swithinbank, Robert Hamilton Dundas, and Granville Hamilton. Maynard wrote to his parents: "Hamilton's latest freak is female dresses. He stayed out for a day and spent the whole time reading fashion articles."

He recorded in his diary that he had been beaten by his Eton master, Chute, and precociously noted the sadomasochistic element: "It gives him a great deal of pleasure and does not do me much harm." Maynard's first sexual intimacy was during his last year at Eton, with Dilwyn Knox, the son of an Evangelical bishop. The two approached the deed in terms of "experimenting" intellectually and sexually with the question "what is necessary to life?" When he told Swithinbank of this, some six years later, Maynard said he had "never seen anyone so surprised and so jealous.... Apparently he had hoped to do likewise himself but never dared, believing it would be absolutely out of the question."

Maynard won the coveted Eton scholarship at King's in both mathematics and classics. However, for all his successes, his social adjustment was impaired by "an unalterable obsession that I am ... physically repulsive.... The idea is so fixed and constant that I don't think anything ... could ever shake it."[4] He entered Cambridge where he would find, as Lytton had, supportive teachers and friends, and through them sexual liberation and a release of creative energy.

One of the most influential younger dons at this time was G. Lowes Dickinson, affectionately known as "Goldie." His book *The Greek View of Life* was highly regarded. In it he presented the Platonic ideal that the highest love was that experienced between two men. He spoke of Cambridge as "the city of friendship and truth," and encouraged many young men. One of these, E. M. Forster, wrote of the university ambiance: "People and books reinforced one

---

[4]*John Maynard Keynes*, by Charles Hession, p. 35.

another, intelligence joined hands with affection, speculation became a passion, and discussion was made profound by love."

Maynard was elected an Apostle in 1903, his candidacy supported by Lytton and Leonard Woolf. His father was overjoyed, noting in his diary: "This is an almost unprecedented distinction for a freshman." His father obviously did not think of the Apostles as a homosexual club. "Although romantic friendships between young men were praised in Greek literature and normal in the public schools, although Socrates' love of Alcibiades was an inspiration to many of the Apostles who loved youthful male beauty, the subject and the practice were rarely brought out into the open before the revolt of the Apostles and the Bloomsberries."[5] Lytton wrote verses teasing Maynard, who was described as:

> *Both penetrating and polite*
> *A liberal and a sodomite,*
> *An atheist and a statistician,*
> *A man of sense, without ambition.*
> *A man of business, without bustle,*
> *A follower of Moore and Russell,*
> *One who, in fact, in every way*
> *Combined the features of the day.*

By fall 1904, Maynard and Lytton dominated the Apostles. Lytton was its secretary and discovered among its papers that one of the traditions was "higher sodomy." They chose "embryos" for more than fine intellect. Arthur Hobhouse was a perfect example of intellect and beauty. He was elected an Apostle. Another candidate appeared, whom Lytton described as "pink and delightful, as embryos should be." This was Edgar "Dicker" Duckworth. Lytton was "rather in love" with him, and expressed his feelings in romantic verse. Inevitably, Maynard was a rival for Dicker and won the battle of who should sponsor him for the Apostles. Maynard also won his affections. Their romance caused such hatred in Lytton that for months he could not bear to see or speak to Maynard.

Eventually, Dicker drifted away from Maynard. Lytton then identified with Maynard's miseries, commiserated with him, and they became fast friends again. They wondered "whether they might not, just possibly, be in love with each other." Allowing for some stormy scenes, and in spite of intense jealousies, the acceptance of sexual encounters with one another and others became a special feature of Bloomsbury friendships.

---

[5]From *The Red and the Blue*, by Andrew Sinclair.

Meanwhile, at Balliol, poor luckless Swithinbank, who had been afraid to experiment at Eton, was in trouble, accused of having improper relations with a millionaire's son, and announced to Lytton and Maynard that he was applying for the post of Inspector General of Brothels in the Fiji Islands. He eventually became a civil servant in Burma.

After leaving Cambridge, Lytton was active as an "angel." He visited whenever possible and on a return visit he met and adored George Mallory, a young mountaineer who later was lost on Mount Everest. Lytton gave up an exciting invitation to Paris in order to have a holiday at Lulworth with fellow-Apostle Rupert Brooke. He failed to meet Lytton's expectations of heavenly perfection. However, brother James Strachey, now at King's, was deeply infatuated with Rupert.

It was another undergraduate organization, however, the Midnight Society, which is considered the nucleus of the Bloomsbury group. Lytton, Clive Bell and Leonard Woolf were exact contemporaries at Cambridge. They formed a reading club with Saxon Sydney-Turner and A. J. Robertson. A sixth member was Thoby Stephen, brother of the beautiful sisters Virginia (who would marry Woolf) and Vanessa (who would marry Bell). Aside from Robertson, whom Lytton had his eye on until he learned his father was a clergyman, and who soon dropped out of the circle, and Thoby, who died at 26, these men remained close friends for the rest of their lives. Unlike the Apostles, this was a conspicuously heterosexual group, although its leader was the fey Lytton.

CLIVE BELL: The Midnight Society met in Clive Bell's rooms in New Court. Clive was the son of a *nouveau riche* family from Wiltshire, whose fortune came from coal. His family was considered pretentious and philistine by most of Clive's intellectual Cambridge friends. This did not trouble him. He heartily enjoyed the privileges of wealth and was devoted to the sporting exercises of his class: hunting (he kept two or three hunters while at university) and shooting, and, a little later, womanizing. He was a *bon vivant* who used his wealth throughout his life as a generous and gracious host. Leonard Woolf described him as an "eager, lively, intensely curious" mind. He was chagrined never to be elected to the Apostles. However, through the Midnight Society, his interest in serious writing bloomed. His interest in art criticism would not develop until later when he spent some time in Paris.

LEONARD WOOLF: Leonard Woolf met Clive Bell at Cambridge, where they became friends. His social background was very different from that of his future brother-in-law. One of nine children in a family of Jewish liberals, he was brought up in a financially tight, puritanical environment.

His father, a barrister, died when Leonard was very young, leaving the family in reduced circumstances. Leonard was able to attend Trinity on a scholarship.

JULIAN THOBY STEPHEN: The Stephen and the Strachey families had long known each other, and Lytton was charmed by Thoby when they met at Cambridge. Lytton wrote to Swithinbank: "He has a wonderful and massive frame, and a face hewn of living rock. His character is as splendid as his appearance.... We call him 'The Goth.'... One day we composed each other's epitaphs. He said that mine should be 'The Universal Exception'; and mine for him was 'The Forlorn Hope.'"

Thoby was the eldest son of Leslie Stephen and belonged to "that same powerful and cultured stratum of the upper-middle class as the Stracheys, and [had] distinguished themselves in many similar spheres—scholastic, legal and military."[6] However, the Stephen home at 22 Hyde Park Gate did not at all enjoy the happy ambiance of the Stracheys'. On the contrary, it became a morbid Victorian environment.

Leslie Stephen enjoyed a productive literary career which included editing the first twenty-six volumes of the *Dictionary of National Biography*. His scholarly pursuits and the domestic tranquility of his first marriage, however, had made him something of a recluse. After his first wife's death, he found himself depressed and in failing health, with a retarded daughter, Laura (b. 1870). His neighbor, Julia Duckworth, was impressed with his literary achievements, and her doting attention became indispensable to him. She was a widow with three children, George (b. 1868), Stella (b. 1869) and Gerald (b. 1870). Leslie Stephen and Julia Duckworth married in 1878. They had four children: Vanessa (b. 1879), Julian Thoby (b. 1880), Virginia (b. 1882) and Adrian (b. 1883).

Even as a little girl, Vanessa assumed a mothering role, giving Thoby, only one year younger than she, his bottle. Virginia early on nicknamed her sister "The Saint." Leslie's first daughter, Laura, in her teens, began to have violent fits and would howl hysterically. Sir Leslie was unsympathetic and referred to her condition as "grotesque waywardness." In 1891 she was permanently placed in a home.

In 1895, at the age of 49, Julia died of influenza. Leslie was plunged into grief and self-pity. He developed the habit of weeping and moaning noisily, and his collapse left him indifferent to his children. Emotional chaos overtook the family. Virginia was emotionally and mentally disturbed by her mother's death, and she is said to have attempted suicide. George Duckworth assumed the position of head of the family and "developed the habit of fondling

---

[6]*Lytton Strachey*, by Michael Holroyd, p. 106.

his half-sisters, confusing sexual attraction with brotherly love. Gerald Duckworth was also, on one occasion, guilty of a sexual offense."[7] Virginia's aversion to sexual intimacy between a man and a woman might stem from George's molestation of her. Vanessa had been allowed to study drawing, and in 1896 she began to attend class three times a day with Arthur Cope, bicycling to his school in South Kensington. It must have been a welcome relief from the melancholia and sexual tensions at home.

Stella Duckworth bore the brunt of her mother's death and her step-father Leslie's collapse. She assumed her mother's role of housekeeper, which included caring for Virginia, who was then suffering from her first bout of madness. Stella escaped from this burdensome position in 1897, through marriage, but died suddenly later that year. Soon after her funeral, Leslie wrote to a friend: "My Vanessa is taking her place as mistress of the house very calmly and will be invaluable."

Vanessa was just twenty when she became responsible for running a large house, and caring for, amongst others, a mad sister, sexually threatening half-brothers, and her tyrannical father, who would be bedridden for the last few months of his life. She undertook the thankless responsibilities of a dutiful Victorian maiden, as housekeeper, bookkeeper, nurse and hostess for her father. She did protest, but in vain, serving as social escort for her rich bachelor half-brother George, who showered her with unwanted gifts and whose physical manifestations of affection revolted her. She would eventually rebel and break all the Victorian rules of conduct.

For the time being, she continued to find solace and diversion in her painting. In 1901, she was accepted into the Painting School of the Royal Academy, where she studied with, among others, John Singer Sargent, then at the height of his career. Although still trapped in the mausoleum that was 22 Hyde Park Gate, relief was on the way, through Thoby's friends from Cambridge. Clive Bell met her during the summer of 1902, and sent some partridges he had shot.

Leslie accepted a knighthood in 1902. His health continued to decline and he died in early 1904. Vanessa inevitably felt a sense of release, but Virginia suffered feelings of guilt which led to her second severe breakdown. She threw herself out of a window, and a nurse was required at all times. While she was convalescing, Vanessa, Thoby and Adrian moved from 22 Hyde Park Gate, S.W.7, to 46 Gordon Square, W.C.1, in the Bloomsbury district of London. As well as a physical escape from their Duckworth stepbrothers, and

---

[7]*Vanessa Bell*, by Frances Spalding, p. 19.

the gloom of their father's house, the move was a symbolic act, their gesture of liberation from Victorian codes of behavior. Even the postal code carried the message: S.W.7 was a suitable residential area for the upper classes while W.C.1 was —off the map. A cabman from smart Kensington was unable to find his way there. It was not a slum, but dowdy and lower middle class in tone. One of its main attractions for the Stephens was that no one they knew lived there, or, they hoped, would come there. They did, however, bring their old cook, Sophie Farrell, along with them.

Soon after they had moved in, young men from Cambridge began to call. Leonard Woolf stopped by, on his way to a post in Ceylon. Lytton came and reported, "Vanessa has to keep her three [sic] mad brothers and sister in control." Saxon Sydney-Turner began to visit regularly. Thoby, anxious to keep in contact with his Cambridge friends, began to be regularly "at-home" on Thursday evenings. Vanessa was "at-home" on Fridays. Clive Bell became a regular visitor and a kind of co-host. He developed an attraction to Vanessa, and proposed marriage to her on two occasions. She rejected him.

Vanessa had no intention of marrying anybody. She was revelling in her newly found freedom. Delightedly, she defied Victorian etiquette, and with Thoby's Cambridge friends as a nucleus she made many men friends, including homosexuals, with whom she could share not only intellectual ideas but also bawdy stories. They were astonished and delighted to find a beautiful young woman who was uncensorious and interested in their secret lives. She could paint on her own schedule. In 1905, she decided to form a club, to be concerned with discussion and exhibitions of paintings. This was the Friday Club, made up of women and men friends from the Royal Academy and the Slade schools, with non-painters allowed in as "lay" members.

Tragedy struck again, however, in 1906, when her beloved brother Thoby died of typhoid fever. In her grief, Vanessa turned to Clive, Thoby's dearest friend. He proposed again, and she accepted. Clive's physical vitality, his wit and intelligence, sense of humor, wealth and sophistication, gave Vanessa a new and happy view of life, and the new experience of having someone looking after her. The marriage was a success sexually and released Vanessa's latent sensuality. She had a new and positive framework for her life. The newlyweds took over the house at 46 Gordon Square (Adrian and Virgina moved to nearby 29 Fitzroy Square).

LADY OTTOLINE MORRELL: Although not accepted by Bloomsbury as one of them, Ottoline was one of many who wanted to be included in that group. She gave to many of them, however, her friendship and useful support. She was a hostess, as well as a source of much amusement to them.

Related to the Duke of Portland, she had been brought up at Welbeck Abbey, one of the great estates of the Dukeries. Although raised in an atmosphere of aristocratic splendor and the country pursuits of the nobility, it was an environment devoid of cultural activities and she received almost no education. She hated her restricted life, and romantically yearned for the society of artists and great minds.

At the age of 29, she married Philip Morrell and in 1905 they set up house, strange to say, in Bedford Square in Bloomsbury, a stone's throw from the British Museum. Here she began to fulfill her dream of being a part of the cultural forces of the time. She entertained on a lavish scale, a variegated group of mostly male guests, from powerful politicians to unknown poets. She had love affairs of various degrees of passion with many of these men, including even Lytton. Of this, Duncan remarked, "Oh, yes, but only hugging and kissing. You see, Ottoline thought she could save Lytton from being a bugger. Lytton used to confide in me." She did have a long-term, intense sexual affair with Bertrand Russell. She was painted by Augustus John, who took her along to one of Virginia's "at-homes" in Fitzroy Square. Ottoline was fascinated by the Bohemian aspects of the scene and made herself an indispensable part of it.

CHAPTER 3

1905–1914

DUNCAN STOPPED ATTENDING the Westminster School of Art in 1905, and rented his own studio in Upper Baker Street. Cousin Pippa Strachey took him to one of Vanessa Stephen's "at-homes," where he met her for the first time. He spent his vacation in France and Wales, and in the autumn lived with his parents, now permanently residing in England at 143 Fellows Road, Hampstead. In August he visited the Stracheys at their rented summer home, Great Oakley Hall, where Lytton was working on his mammoth dissertation on Warren Hastings, a colonial administrator. At that moment, Lytton's romantic interest was focused on Bernard Swithinbank, Maynard's closest friend since their days at Eton. However, on meeting Duncan, the romance with Bernard was cancelled. Lytton told Maynard, "I've managed . . . to catch a glimpse of Heaven. . . . I want to . . . preach an infinitude of sermons on one text—'Embrace one another.' . . . Oh, yes, it's Duncan."

Duncan was soon off to Paris, where he was deluged with letters from Lytton. Lytton suffered great self-pity at the lack of response, and when a letter from Duncan finally arrived he experienced violent indigestion. Lytton begged him to drop everything and come back to Great Oakley Hall for the end of summer. He mentioned that his great friend Maynard Keynes would be there and made the fateful prophecy that Duncan would surely like him. Duncan replied politely, apologizing for not having written sooner and refusing the invitation, saying, "I am afraid I cannot manage it. . . . I should like to have seen Canes (?) [sic] very much." Lytton did manage to introduce Maynard and Duncan that fall.

Lytton's relationship with Duncan progressed and Lytton was very happy. He loved Duncan's new studio, an almost bare room except for the sketches and drawings. Lytton found the work "superb" and had no doubt about Duncan's genius. Duncan would sometimes cook their lunch, making "an omelette in a frying-pan over the fire, and we ate it on the bare wooden table with bread and beer and cheese." In a "Grand Conversation" held in late December 1905, Duncan managed to convince nervous Lytton of his genuine affection and Lytton was ecstatic. As usual, he reported all to Maynard: "All that's obvious and before my nose is that he's absolutely mine. I haven't the nerve to think of the future...." In January, 1906, Lady Colvile invited Lytton and Duncan to stay at her house, Park Cottage, in Hertfordshire, where despite Lytton's conflicting anxieties (Duncan could not have much of a brain if he loved Lytton, etc.), they had a happy week together.

Duncan was very lucky with aunts. As well as Aunt Janie, Aunt Lell (the elegant and cultivated Lady Colvile) looked after him. She gave him £100 for his twenty-first birthday, money to be used to live and study in Paris for a year. On February 18, 1906, accompanied by Lytton, Duncan went to Paris, where they spent the first night at the Hôtel de l'Universe et du Portugal. Also living at the hotel were his friends from the Westminster School of Art, Ballard and Marius Forestier, and his friend Urquart, another Scotsman. They were studying at the Academie Julian. Duncan decided to share rooms with them, in the attic of the hotel.

Lytton gloomily travelled on alone the next day, to Lady Colvile's villa. While at Menton, in the midst of "imbecile dowagers" and "paralyzed old majors," and not an attractive boy in sight, Lytton received a staggering letter. Duncan wrote that "Dicker" Duckworth was with him in Paris and that he had "fallen in love with him and he with me." This was the same Duckworth whom Lytton had lost to Maynard at Cambridge. Duncan said that this new relationship made no difference to his friendship with Lytton and he hoped Lytton would feel the same way. Lytton fell ill as a result, and with a high fever returned to Paris, where his sister Pippa came to take him back to London. "I am rather wrecked," he wrote to Maynard.

Following Simon Bussy's advice, Duncan went to Jacques-Emile Blanche's newly-founded school, La Palette, located near Les Invalides. Blanche was a sophisticated and successful society portraitist, who knew everyone, and painted them: socialites and celebrities of the day such as Colette and Willy, Tamara Karsavina as "The Firebird," Proust in evening clothes, and even Sargent. Blanche was not sympathetic to the Post-Impressionists, and so Duncan was not yet exposed to their work. Even so, Duncan benefited from his work at La Palette, particularly from Blanche's life class, where he pursued his special interest in the nude figure. Duncan remembered Blanche as an intelligent man and a good teacher, who encouraged careful drawing.

Duncan's independent mind always served him. "I never took very much notice of what people said but kept to my instincts and to what I had learned from painters like Piero della Francesca, Masaccio, Chardin, and of course [later on] Cézanne." He visited the Caillebotte Collection which was a revelation to him, particularly its Pissarros and Sisleys, but he was not yet in touch with latest developments in Paris. This was partly because he was so busy, painting in the morning at La Palette, copying after lunch in the Louvre, and after supper, studying anatomy in the library of the École des Beaux Arts; and partly because his circle was still made up mostly of British friends.

Duncan always worked hard at his art, and also led a very energetic life. Marius Forestier's uncle gave the boys some money so they could visit a brothel. There was one, complete with a red light, conveniently next to their hotel. Too shy to go with Marius, Duncan, full of trepidation, went alone. He gave his 18 francs to Madame, pointed to a pretty young girl, and was escorted upstairs, where he manfully enjoyed himself until a tap at the door announced that time was up. He promised to come again if he could raise the money.

In June, Duncan visited Florence and Siena. Back in England for the summer, he continued to enjoy the choicest Apostles, now taking the much admired "Hobby" Hobhouse with him to Rothiemurchus. "Yes, indeed, Arthur Hobhouse," Duncan recalled, "he *was* a Greek god." The two young men were lent a remote guest house on the estate, where Duncan said, "That's where I really got to know him." Duncan liked him "a lot" but after a year and a half their affair ended badly, with Duncan being thrown out of the Hobhouse family house. "He was desperate to keep his mother ignorant of our affair, but my passionate remonstrations and expressions of despair must have reached the butler's ears. Anyway, Hobhouse told me not to visit him again."

Duncan returned for his last term at La Palette in 1907, where Blanche continued to be helpful and admiring. Duncan was now more at home with the French. He moved from the hotel to 22 rue Delambre, and then to a large block of studios at 45 rue Campagne Première, Montparnasse. He spent more time in his own studio, working on larger compositions, often filled with amorous gods and goddesses, inspired by his great new discovery, Poussin. He was introduced to Augustus John by Henry Lamb, and visited the Salon des Indépendents. Another art student in Paris at this time was Wyndham Lewis, who forced himself upon Duncan when they crossed paths at the Café du Dôme. "My gorge simply rises whenever I see him," Duncan wrote to Lytton. Duncan became more sympathetic to Lewis about 1911 when they were both members of the Camden Town Group of painters.

A painter whose company Duncan enjoyed at the time was Maxwell Armfield, then having some success in Paris. Armfield had first noticed

Duncan in the National Gallery in London, when he was copying the angels in Piero della Francesca's "Nativity." Armfield recorded in his diary, "Have seen the most thrilling person. . . . He is exactly a Piero person. I accosted him today and he appears quite delightful—Scotch. . . . his eyes are extraordinarily grey and liquid, very pale, with huge irises and long lashes." In May they visited Chartres to see and paint the Cathedral. Their friendship, however, did not survive aesthetic differences.

On Easter Sunday, Vanessa and Clive Bell arrived in Paris, following their honeymoon in Manorbier. Her brother and sister, Virginia and Adrian, arrived soon after. Lytton had written to Vanessa saying, "Look up my little cousin, when you're in Paris." She did and Duncan dined with all four of them. He was most admiring of Virginia and most fond of Adrian. Maynard Keynes, now working at the India Office in London, also came to Paris for Easter, and stayed with Duncan at rue Delambre. They spent time together, visiting Versailles where Duncan was amused by Maynard's enthusiasm for the splendid fountains.

In June, Duncan finished his last term at La Palette. He went to Florence, and visited I Tatti, the luxurious villa of the art historian and dealer, Bernard Berenson. Leo Stein, Gertrude's brother, was there at the time. Duncan continued his studies of Italian art, visiting Certaldo, San Gimignano, and Siena. He then joined Lytton for a week in Versailles, where they spent much time in the Trianon Gardens. Lytton had been offered his first paying job with the *Spectator*, which the future economist Maynard advised him to accept, saying, "It is hardly possible to overestimate the importance of money."

Returning from Europe in mid-July, 1907, Duncan went to his parents' house in London and then went on to Rothiemurchus. The laird, his cousin John Peter Grant, had commissioned a portrait of, in his own words, his "ugly features." This remarkable painting now hangs in the National Galleries of Scotland. It was an auspicious beginning to Duncan's career as a portrait painter. Duncan would bring the great tradition of English portraiture into the twentieth century. But the years following his return from Paris were difficult. He made two abortive efforts to study at the Slade School of Art, and was often depressed about his work. He exhibited at the United Arts Club in 1907 ("South Porch, Chartres," and "Walnut Trees") but was at first rejected by the New English Art Club, the most progressive group in London at the time.

He took a studio near Belsize Park Gardens and began a series of brilliant portraits of everybody within his reach, including a self-portrait, 1908 (see book jacket). He painted new friends from Cambridge, including Cecil Taylor, 1909; and many relatives, Lytton Strachey, 1909 (Number 37), and Adrian Stephen, 1910, to mention only a few. He painted an atmospheric picture, rather than a portrait, of Marjorie Strachey, which he insisted on calling "Le Crime et le Châtiment," 1909 (Number 36). It shows her holding her head in her hands, overcome by Dostoevsky's novel. He painted another self-portrait, wearing a green turban, in 1910 (Number 46). Originally he painted himself with a strange tall hat, supported by his right hand. Later he painted out the hat, but left his arm in an odd position over his head.[1]

Duncan had a thorough understanding of French and Italian schools of the past, and highly developed technical skills. His technique and versatility are displayed in these portraits, in which his "discreet realism" is already invaded by a conspicuous delight in the flourish and swirl of pattern, and foretell his development as a designer-decorator. He learned from everyone—Corot's portraits, mosaics at Ravenna, portraits from Greco-Roman art. He exhibited two pictures at the 1909 Winter Exhibition of the New English Art Club, one of them his "Portrait of James Strachey" (Number 38). The influence of the Post-Impressionists begins to show in the use of spotted color in Duncan's portrait of G. H. Luce, 1910, in what Vanessa called "Duncan's leopard manner."

Duncan's private life now centered on his lover, Maynard Keynes. (Gwen Darwin Raverat, a member of Vanessa's Friday Club, made an appealing portrait of him at about this time—Number 42.) Their intimacy continued until 1914, and Maynard remained Duncan's greatest friend until his death in 1946. Duncan later told Paul Roche that he found his relationship with Maynard interesting because they were so different from one another. He said he liked "everything" about Maynard, "Everything, but of course his extreme cleverness. And his marked kindness to *me*."

In the summer of 1908, Duncan went to the Orkney Islands, off the north coast of Scotland. He wrote Maynard to tell him that he had discovered the perfect village for a holiday, Rackawick, "where the people are frequently mad from too frequent incest.... There is no priest, no church *and* no policeman. Don't you think we'd better go there at once?" The lovers remained in these remote islands for two months, on their "honeymoon," Lytton bitterly observed.

Romantic as their sojourn was, neither neglected his work. Maynard wrote for hours a day on his "Treatise on Probability" while Duncan drew the landscape and made a beautiful portrait of his friend (Number 43). Once

---

[1]Duncan loved headgear of all sorts. See Number 7, photo with turban, and Number 24, last photo with Paul.

again, Lytton was devastated. Not only was he jealous, but mortified because, not knowing of their love affair, he had been writing to each of them, describing Duncan to Maynard as irresponsible and describing Maynard to Duncan as lacking in passion. Lachrymose letters were exchanged all around.

After the holiday, Maynard returned to Cambridge where he was now a lecturer in economics and Duncan went back to London. Maynard complained of the lack of letters from Duncan. "Why aren't you a Cambridge undergraduate, damn you, instead of a wretched Londoner? Come, and I will make King's Chapel into a studio for you." Maynard was the dependent one, anxious for signs of love from Duncan. Independence was a dominant feature in Duncan's character. His art came first, throughout his life, and he made no secret of it. This disappointed a lot of people who wanted to possess him, but he let no one and nothing interfere with his creative work. He was always very productive, and at this time, 1908-11, in his early twenties, his creative genius was beginning to be recognized, and he was considered a leading contributor to the Post-Impressionist movement in England.

Maynard, despite the fact that he tended "to spend the whole day being in love with" Duncan, was also excited with his own work: "Here are my theories—will statistics bear them out? Nothing except copulating is so enthralling...." He also wrote Duncan that homosexuality had "grown by leaps and bounds" and "practically everybody in Cambridge, except me, is an open and avowed sodomite." The Oscar Wilde case of 1895, with imprisonment, resulting impoverishment, and early death in 1900, was still a subject of interest in this charged atmosphere.

Duncan and Maynard spent the Easter vacation of 1909 in Paris and Versailles. They visited the Salon des Indépendents and the Louvre and saw Sarah Bernhardt in "L'Aiglon." Duncan may have begun his acquaintance with Picasso about this time, when he went to see Gertrude Stein and her collection of work by Matisse, Picasso and others. With an introduction from Simon Bussy, he visited Matisse at Issy-les-Moulineaux. In August and September, Duncan made a studio in a house Maynard had rented in a village near Oxford. Back in London, they shared a flat in Belgrave Road, then moved together to 21 Fitzroy Square, where Duncan had a studio on the first floor. Adrian and Virginia lived in the same square. Duncan visited them often, particularly attracted to Adrian, whom he painted many times.

Vanessa Bell had by this time given birth to her first child, Julian (b. 1908), and experienced disillusion with her husband, who during her pregnancy had been lured into a flirtation by her jealous sister Virginia. "If gradually their love for each other evaporated, it distilled into a lasting affection. . . . For the rest of his life, while never ceasing to admire his wife, [Clive] was never without a mistress."[2]

A core group of friends was now established through the "at-homes" in Bloomsbury. "Their bawdiness, if anything, increased when in the summer of 1908 sexual inversion flourished like German measles. H.T.J. Norton [the mathematician] fell momentarily in despair over James Strachey who was besotted with Rupert Brooke; Lytton was distraught because Duncan had fallen in love with Keynes. . . . " In her father's house, "power, action and creativity had seemed [to Vanessa] a male prerogative; but in the company of these intellectuals, a less obviously masculine approach to life seemed to encourage sensitivity, imagination and wit."[3] (Virginia Woolf considers the question of androgyny and creativity in her book *A Room of One's Own*.[4])

Vanessa gained confidence in her painting and sent pictures to the Allied Artists Exhibition and to the New English Art Club, which had been founded as an alternative to the Royal Academy. Her still life "Iceland Poppies" (this painting can be seen on the wall behind Paul Roche,—Number 16) was exhibited by them, and Duncan praised it in one of his rare reviews, in the *Spectator.*

Throughout his long life, Duncan loved dressing up. In a photo, taken when he was about six years old, he appears as Cupid. In February 1910, Duncan participated in the "Dreadnought Hoax," an escapade arranged by Horace de Vere Cole with Adrian Stephen. A telegram which appeared to be from the Foreign Office was received at the Admiralty, alerting the First Lord that the Emperor of Abyssinia and retinue were en route to Weymouth and desired to inspect the biggest and newest of His Majesty's ships of line, the Admiral's flagship *HMS Dreadnought.* The "royal party" consisted of Cole, Adrian and Virginia, Duncan, and two friends.

Heavily made up in black face and moustaches, and dressed by Clarksons, the theatrical costumers, they proceeded by train from Paddington and were welcomed with a red carpet. "A smart little brass-funnelled launch took us out to the Dreadnought," Duncan recalled. "Adrian was nervous because the Admiral was a cousin of his, and then to his horror the Captain . . . turned out to be someone he knew very well and used to go on long walks with. But he wasn't recognized. . . . " The sailors were paraded and inspected, the band played the anthem of Zanzibar, and decorations were

---

[2]*Vanessa Bell*, by Frances Spalding, pp. 77-78.

[3]*Vanessa Bell*, by Frances Spalding, pp. 78-79.

[4]See *Toward a Recognition of Androgyny*, by Carolyn Heilbrun.

offered. "Adrian did most of the speaking . . . . mispronouncing whole passages of Homer and Virgil which he'd had to learn by heart as a boy and mixing it up with a few words of Swahili."

Cole, "out for publicity, let the cat out of the bag. There was quite a stir . . . headlines, questions asked in the House, music-hall songs, and the Navy furious. They proceeded to punish us each in turn." While Duncan was sitting at breakfast with his parents, the maid announced that some gentlemen had called to see him. He went to the door in his slippers. There were three young Naval officers, each carrying a cane, who bundled Duncan into a cab. They took him to a field "and I did whatever I was told. . . . It all ended by their giving me two ceremonial taps on the behind. The honor of the Navy was seen to be vindicated and that was that."[5]

Maynard was involved in politics during the winter of 1909-10, writing and speaking in support of the liberal cause. For Easter vacation, he and Duncan were off again, this time for an adventurous trip to Greece and Constantinople. In Athens, their room looked out on the Acropolis and the Temple of Theseus. Maynard early on began collecting Duncan's work. "On the Acropolis," 1910, is now in the Keynes' Collection at Cambridge. Maynard, as well as studying Adam Smith's *The Wealth of Nations*, took photographs of nude sculpture for Duncan. They travelled with a dragoman who cooked for them; Maynard's wallet was stolen; they saw whirling dervishes in Turkey and shared an exciting time. "I wonder if you realize how immensely happier I was than if you had not been with me," Maynard later wrote to Duncan.

With Maynard working in Cambridge, Duncan, never one to suffer solitude, went out with other young men and in particular began seeing a lot of Adrian Stephen, which caused gossip and hurt Maynard. Vanessa wrote to her sister, "I am somewhat skeptical about the great passion" between her brother Adrian and Duncan. She would remain skeptical about Duncan's passions for the next fifty years.

Duncan has described the Thursday evenings in Adrian's study in Fitzroy Square: " . . . a continuation of those evenings which began in Gordon Square before Thoby died and Vanessa married. It was there that what has been called 'Bloomsbury' for good or ill came into being." People arrived between ten and midnight and stayed until two or three in the morning. "Whisky, buns and cocoa were the diet, and people talked to each other. If someone had lit a pipe he would sometimes hold out the lighted match to Hans the dog, who would snap at it and put it out. Conversation; that was all."

---

[5]*With Duncan Grant in Southern Turkey*, by Paul Roche, pp. 34-36.

The year 1910 was an important one in the history of art in England, thanks to Roger Fry. He was at the height of his eminence as an art critic when he met Clive and Vanessa. The three of them became instant friends. He was excited by the work Vanessa and Duncan were doing; and Vanessa and Clive helped him mount the controversial and highly influential first Post-Impressionist Exhibition, which included work by Van Gogh, Gauguin and Cézanne. Although Roger was older than they were, there seemed no gap in their views on painting. Roger was folded into the Bloomsbury set and became their most articulate spokesman, publicist and patron. It was his concern for these artists as well as aesthetic goals that inspired him to set up the Omega Workshops, in 1913.

At the age of twenty-five, Duncan's career began to take off. He showed three pictures in June in the Friday Club's exhibition held at the Alpine Club, including "Lemon Gatherers" (now in the Tate Gallery), inspired by the Sicilian Players, seen at the Shaftesbury Theatre. Vanessa wrote to Clive, "I was very much impressed by it and really think that he may be going to be a great painter." She wrote the next day to tell Clive she had bought it. He also exhibited again in the Winter Exhibition of the New English Art Club. He had been very impressed by the Post-Impressionist Show, particularly by the work of Cézanne. Duncan's still life, "Peaches," 1910 (now in the Courtauld Institute), is one of his first canvasses which shows the powerful impact Cézanne made on him.

In a letter dated 15 November 1910, Clive told Duncan that he was "rapidly becoming celebrated." In February, 1911, Duncan's "Idyll" was shown at the Friday Club. During these years, Duncan worked on murals commissioned by Maynard for his rooms at Webb Court, King's College, Cambridge (Number 50). Painted directly on the walls, four of the panels represent grape pickers. In theme and execution, these are related to "Lemon Gatherers." Duncan had difficulty with Keynes' murals. At one point he threw down his brushes in frustration and burst into tears. He never considered them finished, and after the war he and Vanessa redecorated Keynes' rooms, replacing them with new work (Number 51).

Vanessa's life in 1910 was taken up with looking after others. She was pregnant with her second child when Virginia suffered a return of her mental illness. After several months of unsuccessful effort to help her, Vanessa was concerned to find someone to care for Virginia before she herself went into labor. Virginia was put in a private nursing home, which she deeply resented and where she again threatened to kill herself. "Clarissa," Vanessa's second child, born in August, 1910, turned out to be a boy. He was renamed Gratian, a name no one liked. Clive, a Victorian gentleman in his revulsion at the nastiness inevitable with infancy, fled. At this time, Vanessa wrote to her husband, of his mistress Mrs. Raven-Hill, "I hope you'll see your whore soon."

Saxon Sydney-Turner spent some time with Vanessa and concentrated on working through Latin dictionaries and the index to Gibbon, looking for a new name for the baby: "Viggo Bell, Pausanias Bell, Crippen...." Claudian was used, for a time, but he was eventually called Quentin. Duncan visited Vanessa during her convalescence and she wrote to Clive: "We talked mostly about painting as we could not discuss any really improper subjects freely..." in the presence of a lady visitor.

In spring 1911, Vanessa and Clive, with Roger Fry and Harry Norton, took the Orient Express to Turkey. (Just before leaving London, Roger had been surprised to find himself in bed with Lady Ottoline.) On the trip, Vanessa and Roger began to enjoy being together, painting together. Vanessa was pregnant again, and this interlude was interrupted when she suffered a miscarriage, followed by a complete physical breakdown. With the grim example of her sister in her mind, she feared she was going mad. Her husband was frantic with concern, while Roger, kind and gentle and experienced in nursing his own mentally ill wife, sat with her throughout the nights and reassured her that she would get better. She did, but it was several years before her health was fully restored.

Back in England, she lived an invalid's life, and during the summer took lodgings at Millmead Cottage, Guildford, to be near Roger. She managed to manufacture a quarrel between Roger and Lady Ottoline, ending their brief affair. Vanessa and Roger kept their affair a secret from Clive.

She was in London at the time of the coronation of George V and wrote to Roger: "Duncan... thought it very beautiful, with... charming Chinamen lolling back in their carriages smoking cigarettes.... The Duchess of Devonshire's footman was the most exquisite creature he had ever seen. Also the Prince of Wales stirred him a little! He doesn't seem to be changing his tastes very quickly, does he?" Vanessa was loath to accept that Duncan would never change his "tastes." She told Roger that she and Duncan had decided to emulate the artist Eric Gill "and paint really indecent subjects. I suggest a series of copulations in strange attitudes and have offered to pose. Will you join? I mean in the painting. We think there ought to be more indecent pictures around." Duncan did enjoy creating erotica, as most creative artists do, and drew and painted beautiful and imaginative pictures. His erotic work is remarkable for its absence of violence and its pure sensuality, unsullied by any kind of sexism (Frontispiece).

In the same letter, Vanessa goes on to tell Roger how she wants to talk to him and read his work. She was obviously wonderfully in love with him. Frances Spalding wrote, "Though her marriage had been a success, it was Roger who fully unleashed Vanessa's sexual passion."

While the Bells had been abroad with Roger, Maynard and Duncan had visited Sicily and Tunis. Their love affair was not going well. Maynard was disappointed that Duncan seemed sad and did not show much open affection for him, and in Naples they had a terrible row. Maynard sent Duncan away, but they were soon reconciled. On their way home, they stopped in Florence at I Tatti.

Back in London, Maynard was thrilled with Serge Diaghilev's Ballets Russes and often went to see them. Duncan was plunged into new work, thanks to Roger Fry. Roger, himself a gifted painter and decorator, had been invited by his old friend from Cambridge, Basil Williams, to devise a decoration for the students' dining room at the Borough Polytechnic near the Elephant and Castle. He invited Duncan and a number of young artists to join him, notably Frederick Etchells and his sister Jessie, also a painter, who were already members of the Friday Club.

The theme for the decoration was "London on Holiday," and it was Duncan and Frederick who discussed plans to give the individual murals some unity. Duncan chose "Football" (Number 41) and "Bathing" (Number 40) as his subjects (both are now in the Tate Gallery), Frederick Etchells "The Fair," Roger Fry "The Zoo," Bernard Adeney "Sailing Boats," Albert Rutherston "Paddlers," and MacDonald Gill "Punch and Judy."

The students did not like the decoration of their dining room but, typical of Roger's ventures, the murals had wide coverage in the press. To Roger's delight, the *National Review* wrote, "the perpetrators of these travesties are more to be pitied than to be blamed."

Duncan emerged the star of the undertaking, and from then on was considered the most promising young artist of the English Post-Impressionists. The *Spectator* reserved its praise for "Bathing," mentioning "...Signorelli figures arching themselves like great bows in the foreground...the figure scrambling into the boat in the background is a noble piece of draughtmanship...gives an extraordinary impression of the joys of lean athletic life. It makes one want to swim—even in water like an early Christian mosaic." *The Times* agreed and said the painting represented the act of swimming, rather than individual swimmers, "in the morning of the world. All the colour of the painting, arbitrary as it appears, is equally expressive and conveys the same feeling."

"Duncan Grant's murals in c.1911 were considerably more advanced than his easel painting at that time. The opportunity to design on a large scale released a formal inventiveness which had previously been confined to sketches and drawings of figures in the manner of Poussin and Rubens."[6] Roger also commissioned Duncan to do a mural in the entrance hall of his house, Durbins, near Guildford.

Duncan now began to exhibit more widely. Edward Marsh, private secretary and close friend of Winston Churchill, whom Raymond Mortimer called "the greatest friend that our painters and poets have found in the twentieth century," bought Duncan's "Parrot Tulips" from the Second Camden Town Group Exhibition of December, 1911.

Around this time, he painted a remarkable picture of a woman bathing, and made several versions of it over the next years (Number 47). In 1912 his "The Red Sea—Decoration" attracted favorable notice at the Friday Club; "Idyll" and "Lemon Gatherers" were shown by the Contemporary Art Society in Manchester; he was included in "Quelques Indépendents Anglais," at the Galerie Barbazanes, Paris; and showed six pictures in Roger Fry's Second Post-Impressionist Exhibition, Grafton Galleries. Roger bought Duncan's semi-pointillist picture "The Queen of Sheba," whose background camels were done from sketches and photos made in Tunis in 1911, and sold it to the Contemporary Art Society, which exhibited it widely. H. Granville-Barker, the actor-producer, commissioned Duncan to design a production of *Hamlet*, but the project was not realized.

In 1912, Duncan had a painting holiday in Granchester with Jacques Raverat and Rupert Brooke. Maynard went with Gerald Shove to the Riviera. In July, Maynard booked the entire Crown Hotel, in Everleigh, a place he had discovered on a riding trip, and invited all his friends to join him there. Perhaps two dozen men and women came, including his brother Geoffrey, Duncan, Gerald Shove, Dilly Knox, Rupert Brooke, Justin Brooke (no relation), the Olivier sisters, Katherine Cox, G. H. Luce, and Ferenc Békássy, a young nobleman from Budapest in whom Maynard was interested. The landlady was shocked by the guests' behavior and charged an extra £40 "blood money." Maynard himself was horrified to see Rupert Brooke making love to a member of the opposite sex. This holiday was to be remembered with

[6]*Bloomsbury Portraits*, by Richard Shone, p. 69.

nostalgic pleasure by all as a symbol of the peaceful and cultivated life-style destroyed forever by the First World War.

In October, Duncan made his first trip abroad with his new friends, Roger and Clive, on a tour of France. Back in London, he and Maynard moved into the Stephens' house. Duncan and Maynard had the ground floor; Adrian the first; Virginia the second; Gerald Shove, the economist, was fitted in somewhere; and Leonard Woolf, back from Ceylon and in love with Virginia, was on the top floor.

Duncan began to paint startling pictures directly on the walls of the rooms. One, called "Street Accident," was painted with Frederick Etchells. In Adrian's rooms, Duncan painted a tennis game (Number 49). The figures are simplified shapes which pre-figure Matisse's dancers in the Barnes Foundation and the gouache cut-outs of his last years.[7] They seem as much dancers as athletes and reflect Duncan's new experience with the ballet. Indeed, Duncan's love of the masculine figure made him use sports, dance and love-making as points of departure to entangle bodies, but in any setting color and line were of equal concern (Numbers 50, 58, 59, 86, 87, 88, 89).

Diaghilev's Ballets Russes first was in London during the time of the coronation of King George V, and returned often, until the war made travel impossible. Serge Diaghilev assembled the greatest dancers, composers and artists to create the ultimate ballet company. Among his discoveries and stars were the legendary Nijinsky, Karsavina, Fokine, Stravinsky, Debussy, Bakst, and Picasso. The Ballets Russes was an enormous success and had great and lasting influence on all the arts.

Lady Ripon and other smart hostesses vied to entertain Diaghilev, who was especially interested in Lady Ottoline, because of her connections with the English avant garde. She invited Vaslav Nijinsky to Bedford Square, where Duncan came to meet him. When he entered the drawing room, Duncan heard Lady Ottoline asking Nijinsky, sitting next to her: "Aimez-vous Platon?" It was with considerably more interest that Nijinsky and Leon Bakst watched Duncan play tennis in the garden. "Nijinsky, seeing the ballet/ of tennis players in white/ darting between the tall, theatrical/ and sepia-mottled columns of the vaulting trees,/ threw out a dancer's arm, and called/ in a faun's warm voice/ 'Ah, quel décor!'"[8]

---

[7]The house was destroyed by German bombs in 1940.

[8]From "The Plane Trees of Bedford Square," by William Plomer, printed as a pamphlet by Jonathan Cape Ltd., in 1971.

The scene was the inspiration for Nijinsky's ballet *"Jeux,"* 1913, with music by Debussy.[9] Bakst's decor was of "dreaming garden trees," half concealing the facade of Bedford Square.[10] Duncan remembered in his final days his frustrated desire to design a ballet for Nijinsky.[11]

Duncan's fascination with the dancer never ceased (Numbers 67 and 68) and he kept the famous Druet photograph of Nijinsky (Number 66) in his studio all his life.[12] In 1972, he painted "Still Life with Nijinsky," incorporating the photograph into the painting. (Leon Bakst also made a painting from this photograph.)

Maynard (who was devoted to the Diaghilev Ballet and would marry a ballerina, the fabulous Lydia Lopokova, after the war) had become by 1912 a Cambridge don, editor of the Royal Economic Society's journal and was about to become a member of the Royal Commission on the Indian Currency. Not yet thirty years old, he was already a respected authority in his controversial field. During 1908-12, he had suffered unusual depression and anxiety over his relationship with Duncan. In 1912, however, he wrote to the young artist that his "state of mind has become much more peaceable....I am horribly engulfed [in work] at Cambridge." He seems to have found relief from emotional problems through the hard work which made him the most famous economist of the twentieth century. "At several notable crises...World War I, the Great Depression..., and in the financing and economic management of World War II and its aftermath, the British relied heavily on Keynes to diagnose and deal with enormously complex financial and economic problems."[13] He was always Duncan's good friend and he was fast becoming a very powerful patron.

---

[9]In his diary, Nijinsky wrote: *"Jeux* is the life of which Diaghilev dreamed. He wanted to have two boys as lovers. In the ballet, the two girls [danced by Karsavina and Shollar] represent the boys and the young man [danced by Nijinsky] is Diaghilev."

[10]*Nijinsky,* by Richard Buckle, p. 259.

[11]Duncan Grant told the author that Diaghilev told Duncan that he would have been a great dancer, and also that Diaghilev had invited him to design a tennis ballet for Nijinsky but the war intervened. Duncan was telescoping several memories. *Jeux* was created before the war. In 1918, Roger Fry discussed with Diaghilev the possibility of Duncan designing a ballet but unfortunately nothing came of it.

[12]It was Jacques-Emile Blanche, Duncan's first teacher in Paris, who had commissioned Druet to take a series of photos of Nijinsky in costume for the ballet Danses Siamoise, in 1910.

[13]*John Maynard Keynes,* by Charles Hession, p. 93.

CHAPTER 4

The Omega Workshops

THE CONCEPT OF AN ARTISTS' WORKSHOP for decorative and applied art had been of interest to Roger Fry (1866-1934) for many years. But he was not interested in participating in already existing groups, and evaded the invitation to join his friend Charles Robert Ashbee's Guild of Handicraft, which was based on the Ruskin-Morris pattern. Fry would wait and eventually put together a group of artists whose aesthetic would be basically antithetical to the ideals of the craft guilds, with their emphasis on expensive material, technical perfection and the subordination of design to function. As in his life in general, in creating the Omega Workshops this brilliant and energetic man had multiple ambitions and motivations.

A gifted painter who did not despise the decorative arts, Roger designed book plates for such discriminating clients as Bernard Berenson; did book illustration; designed some furniture for the Cambridge rooms of his schoolfriend, the philosopher McTaggart; designed a drawing room frieze for the poet Robert Trevelyan; and painted murals for the drawing room of C.R. Ashbee's mother in Cheyne Walk. In 1900 he wrote to Trevelyan that he loved working within the limits of decoration and wished he could do more, adding, "Why won't the architects use me?" However, his ambitions for a workshop went far beyond the need of a vehicle for personal expression. Not long after the death of Queen Victoria, he determined to undertake no less a crusade than the radical alteration of bourgeois preconceptions of art and the relationship of art to interior decoration, and indeed to all other aspects of daily life.

By his early thirties, Roger Fry had become a respected Victorian scholar and authority on Italian Renaissance art. He was an establishment figure, consultant for a time to the Metropolitan Museum of Art in New York City, an appointment terminated in 1910 due to a dispute with J. P. Morgan, then the Museum's chairman. In middle age, he was to abandon, with great glee, a secure position, to become the bad boy of the British art establishment. Among the many ideas Roger had assimilated from France was the *épater la bourgeoisie* technique of gaining attention. He dubbed his self-confident and self-satisfied countrymen "Custard Islanders," "the inhabitants of Bird's Custard Island." (Bird's Custard was and indeed still is a popular brand of bland, inexpensive, easy-to-prepare pudding sauce.)

To dramatize for the British public a new way of seeing, Roger organized an exhibition of contemporary French paintings, which he presented in the winter of 1910, at the Grafton Galleries in London. This was "Manet and the Post-Impressionists." Included were paintings by Cézanne, Derain, Gauguin, Matisse, Picasso, Rouault, Vlaminck and Van Gogh. It caused the desired scandal and outrage, and the term Post-Impressionist, coined for this occasion by Fry, entered the vocabulary of art history. It had some of the same cultural shock value the appearance of Diaghilev's Ballets Russes created in Paris in 1909. Roger's exhibition was a landmark in the history of art in Britain, and things were never to be the same again.

In the winter of 1912, he presented a second Post-Impressionist exhibition, again at the Grafton Galleries. However, this exhibition included, as well as French and Russian work, paintings by young English artists, with Duncan Grant, Vanessa Bell, Wyndham Lewis and Frederick Etchells represented. The public and the art establishment, as embodied by the Royal Academy, were once again violently outraged. Henry Tonks, only a few years older than Fry and a teacher at the Slade School of Art, used work in these exhibitions as examples of contamination his students should avoid. Lytton Strachey wrote, in a letter to the *Nation,* in February 1913: "Nobody could be surprised if a stake were set up tomorrow for Mr. Roger Fry in the courtyard of Burlington House (the home of the Royal Academy)."

As well as his ambition to be arbiter of taste and lead the way into the twentieth century, to the New Jerusalem of Art, Roger enjoyed the friendship of those artists whose work so excited and animated him, and he wanted to help support them financially as well as critically. Older than most of them, Roger was also more financially secure, and this, along with his intellectual authority, gave him a kind of father-figure role which did not displease him. He was concerned that many artists, especially those outside the Academy, could not support themselves through their work.

Pamela Diamond, Roger's daughter, remembers that in the hot summer of 1911 her father had commissioned Henri Doucet, the French painter, and Duncan Grant to come to his house in Guildford to do her portrait. The plan got off to a bad start because Duncan appeared three days late. Questioned, Duncan finally admitted that he hadn't come because he hadn't the one shilling and sixpence for the fare. Finally, he had found a florin in the back of a drawer and was able to come. (Duncan's portrait of Pamela (Number 39) was one of the most highly praised pictures in the 1912 Grafton Exhibition.) This incident must have provoked Roger's concern to create a workshop which could provide at least a modest livelihood for artists. The Omega Workshops would be this device.

Roger's marriage was tragically marred by his wife's recurring mental illness. She was permanently committed to an institution in 1910. Although he cared for her devotedly, he had many friendships, flirtations and love affairs. In 1911, he fell in love with Vanessa Bell who reciprocated his love with a sexual passion she had not known before. Her later obsession with Duncan Grant, who unabashedly preferred men as lovers, caused Roger deep unhappiness, and confusion all around. In the best Bloomsbury style, Roger continued to be a loyal friend to both Duncan and Vanessa, just as Vanessa's husband Clive did. The beginning of Roger's love affair with Vanessa slightly preceded the founding of the Omega Workshops and must have given him added inspiration for that enormously complicated project.

In December 1912, Roger faced the practical problems of making his dream a working reality. He wrote to Wyndham Lewis that he was "horribly busy... working very hard to raise the capital for our decorative scheme." He sent a long circular letter describing his plan for the workshops to a number of persons, including George Bernard Shaw and Clive Bell's wealthy father: "I am intending to start a workshop for decorative and applied art. I find that there are many young artists whose painting shows strong decorative feeling, who will be glad to use their talents on applied art both as a means of livelihood and as an advantage to their work as painters and sculptors." He used the name Omega for the first time, outlined his plans and asked for financial support.

There was objection to the name from Roger's Quaker family, for its strong Christian connotations: "I am Alpha and Omega, the beginning and the ending... the first and the last" (Revelation i, 8 and 11). However, Roger wanted a trademark to protect the Workshops' designs. The name Omega was useful as it was both a word and a symbol; and despite criticism, he stuck with his choice.

By the end of December, George Bernard Shaw had sent £250, a considerable sum in 1912. Roger soon raised the rest of the capital and took a lease on 33 Fitzroy Square for the Omega Workshops. In April 1913, Roger, Vanessa and Duncan produced designs for printed linens. On May 13, Roger and Duncan signed articles of association for the Omega Workshops Limited, witnessed by Clive and Vanessa Bell, and the next day it was formally registered as a limited company with a capital of £1000 in £1 shares. Duncan was assigned one share.

The basic idea of the Omega Workshops was that there would be a place where artists could work together manufacturing and decorating a great variety of household objects—furniture, pottery, and textiles—conceived in a modern spirit.[1] Their products were to be made anonymously, with only the Omega mark to identify the source. This was also to be a meeting place for ideas. Spontaneity was encouraged. The hope and goal was to establish an entirely new idiom in decorative art. The artists were to be at the Workshops no more than three and a half days a week, not be distracted from their more serious creative work, and they were to be paid seven shillings and sixpence a day.

Anything they wished to work on was acceptable, from pencil boxes, fire screens, woolwork chaircovers, table runners, lamp shades, rugs, screens, painted tables and fabric designs to major interior design schemes. No one seems to have told the artists what to do. They kept casual hours. There were non-artists as staff and helpers to keep things going on a slightly more business-like basis. One of Duncan's first contributions was a painted screen (Number 27).

Frederick Etchells painted a table, and Duncan, Vanessa and Clive designed printed linens, which were produced at the Maromme Print Works in France.[2]

Roger counted on the patronage of fashionable London hostesses he knew and Lady Ottoline Morrell, Lady Cunard, Lady Drogheda and Lady Desmond all became customers. A printed linen, "Mechtilde" (probably designed by Etchells), was named after the wife of the German Ambassador, Princess Lichnowsky, who was a patron until she had to leave the country when war broke out. The Workshops' first major undertaking was for the Ideal Home Show of 1913, sponsored by the *Daily Mail*. Omega installed a "Post-

---

[1]Excellent books describing the Omega Workshops are *The Omega Workshops*, by Judith Collins, 1984; *Omega and After, Bloomsbury and the Decorative Arts*, by Isabelle Anscombe, 1981; and the catalogue of the Crafts Council Exhibition of 1984, "The Omega Workshops."

[2]In addition to the Grafton Group artists—Clive, Duncan, Vanessa, Frederick and Wyndham Lewis—some twenty others were associated in one way or another at one time or another with the Workshops, including: Henri Gaudier-Brzeska, the American E. McKnight Kauffer, Paul Nash, David Bomberg, Mark Gertler, Henri Doucet, Nina Hamnett, and Etchells' sister Jessie.

Impressionist room": a sitting room with hand-dyed cushions, printed curtains, and upholstery.

Wyndham Lewis claimed this commission was meant for himself and that Fry had stolen it for Omega. He made this and other charges against Fry in a letter which he sent to everyone associated with the Workshops. The letter was signed by Lewis, Etchells, Cuthbert Hamilton and Edward Wadsworth, who all quit the Omega Workshops. "Lewis' tactics were those of invective, struggle, rebellion and performance and were based upon his theory of art: there was to be no romantic gazing at art, only passionate involvement with it deep in the vortex."[3] Lewis went on his way, to develop his Vorticist movement. There seems to have been no truth to his charges, which had more to do with jealousy and creating a stir.

Omega continued to present work in its showrooms, arranging special exhibitions; for example, a nursery and model bedroom. They had just received a commission to decorate the Cardena Café when war was declared in August 1914. Duncan designed three jointed puppets for a performance of Racine's *Bérenicé*, given at the Workshops. Vanessa initiated the idea that the Omega make women's dresses. The war began to be felt. Friends and colleagues began to die at the front. Roger spent time in France, working for the Quaker War Victims' Relief.

The Omega Workshops continued throughout the war, publishing, exhibiting, and even designing for theatre. However, their momentum and reasons for being were dissipated. Roger was hurt when Vanessa ended their affair and committed herself to Duncan. Duncan's name was now established on its own. In a time of leisure and prosperity, Omega might have prospered, but with the war, Post-Impressionism ceased to be a news item. The Workshops had not made money, and Roger, an artist in his own right, had borne the financial and administrative concerns of the organization. He himself had other, more creative interests to pursue. In March 1919, the sorry state of Omega's finances was presented by Mr. Paice, the accountant, and it was agreed to go into voluntary liquidation. The Omega aesthetic continued, however, and developed in the decorative work of Vanessa and Duncan. Their house, Charleston, in Sussex, became its epitome.

The Omega Workshops were an important part of Duncan's life and released his flair for color and design, but his work also expanded independent of them. In 1913, he began exhibiting with the Grafton Group. He attended the founding meeting of the London Group, and was in group shows in

---

[3]*Omega and After,* by Isabelle Anscombe, p. 34.

Liverpool, Leicester, Manchester, and at the Whitechapel Gallery in London. He was now something of a celebrity in his own right. Duncan had important commissions now. He painted "Adam and Eve" for Clive Bell. In Paris in 1913, he visited Picasso, and Jacques Copeau, one of the most important young directors (and a founder with André Gide of the *Nouvelle Revue Française*), commissioned him to design costumes and scenery for *Twelfth Night*, to be presented at the Théâtre du Vieux Colombier in Paris, an indication of Duncan's standing with the French avant garde.

Duncan, Vanessa and Roger worked on mural decorations for Henry Harris' house in Bedford Square and Ethel Sands' in Chelsea. Duncan executed his remarkable "Abstract Kinetic Collage Painting With Sound," 1914 (Number 48), a non-representational scroll over fourteen feet long. It was meant to be viewed as it was unrolled to the accompaniment of music by Bach. Richard Shone calls this piece "a pioneering work in European abstraction." During this period, Duncan was doing many abstractions and making use of collage. For the Vorticist exhibition of 1915, he sent a "Still Life" and two non-figurative works, with pieces of firewood attached.

In 1912, Virginia married Leonard Woolf and Asheham, their house in Sussex, became a focal point for the Bloomsbury friends. In 1913, Duncan joined Vanessa, Clive and Roger for a trip to Italy, and that summer, Duncan joined Vanessa and Clive on a camping trip at Brandon, in Norfolk. Here Vanessa, beyond enjoying Duncan's company and admiring him as an artist, began to feel a strong physical attraction to him. As she had with Roger, she now found she liked nothing better than to paint, side by side, with Duncan. She would spend most of her life concerned with maintaining that relationship. She, of course, knew he led an active homosexual life and she knew of his relationship with her brother Adrian, with whom he was then living.

At the same time, Duncan's fancy was captured by George Mallory, who, all agreed, was a living work of art "in the Botticelli style...unspoilt by overdevelopment in any part," wrote Maynard, with, according to Lytton, "the body of an athlete by Praxiteles." George is remembered through Duncan's paintings and photographs of him and as one of the mountaineers who died mysteriously near the summit of Mount Everest in 1924. (Duncan had jokingly suggested accompanying him as that expedition's artist.) In 1913, Duncan joined him on a climbing expedition, at Pen-y-Pass, Snowdonia.

Duncan spent Christmas on the Riviera with Maynard, exhausted from his work with the Royal Commission, and went on to Tunis. In May 1914, Vanessa accompanied Duncan to Paris for the première of Copeau's *Twelfth Night*. In July 1914, George Mallory married, and in August the war broke out.

Then, confirming Duncan's apprehension, Adrian Stephen married Karin Costelloe.[4] Losing two favorites at the same time depressed him. "It was at this point that Duncan drew closer to Vanessa and told her that to some extent he returned her love. Those nearest to Vanessa...must have thought it highly unlikely that an intimate relationship between her and Duncan would last....Confronted with Vanessa's feelings Duncan ought to have shied away in terror: that he did not tells us much about Vanessa."[5] Duncan left Brunswick Square and moved in with Vanessa and Clive Bell, at 46 Gordon Square, taking a studio at 22 Fitzroy Street.

For Christmas 1914, Duncan went to stay with Lytton, at The Lacket, near Marlborough, where he encountered David "Bunny" Garnett, seven years his junior, and in a few weeks they had become lovers. As has come to be expected of Duncan's men friends, he was exceptionally good looking and bi-sexual (Numbers 44 and 45). In April, Clive, Vanessa, Duncan and Bunny went to stay at Eleanor House, the home of Mary and St. John Hutchinson (Clive had just begun an affair with Mary Hutchinson).

---

[4]Daughter of Mary Berenson by her first marriage.

[5]*Vanessa Bell*, by Frances Spalding, pp. 133-34.

CHAPTER 5

Wartime and the Move to Charleston

ALL BLOOMSBURY WERE OPPOSED for one reason or another to the war. Lady Ottoline's husband, Philip Morrell, had "spoken out in the House of Commons, a single brave voice, against our entering the war. It was an act of both courage and political suicide. Neither the House nor his constituents wanted any more of him. But at least he could at Garsington [his country house] provide work on the farm for Ottoline's [conscientious objector] friends and many, like Clive, took refuge there."[1]

The war was not, as the public had expected, over by Christmas, and in 1915 the first fears of conscription were felt. True conditions at the front were becoming generally known as the maimed and shell-shocked returned home and death tolls rose. Omega artists Doucet and Gaudier-Brzeska were killed. For failing to register as an alien, Nina Hamnett's Norwegian husband Roald Kristian was sentenced to hard labor and then deported to France. On 23 April 1915, Rupert Brooke died in the Dardanelles. His younger brother Alfred had been killed in action a month earlier. In memory of the two brothers, Duncan painted an abstract work, "In Memoriam: Rupert Brooke," 1915 (Number 52).

The war machine was in motion and unstoppable. Clive wrote a pacifistic pamphlet, *Peace at Once*, which the Lord Mayor ordered destroyed. James Strachey was fired by his cousin St. Loe from the *Spectator* because of his pacifist views. As a Quaker, Roger was immune, and in any case was 50 years old. Duncan, Vanessa, Adrian, David Garnett, and others worked for a time for the National Council of Civil Liberties. Clive and Adrian took up farm work to gain immunity from national service.

Lytton was called up before a tribunal which would consider his exemption plea. He arrived with innumerable brothers and sisters, and other

---

[1] *The Loving Friends*, by David Gadd, p. 113.

"attendant spirits." He inflated a rubber cushion before sitting down on the wooden bench (he was ill and suffering from piles), wrapped himself in a tartan travelling rug and faced the hostile panel, whose military representative asked him what he would do if he saw a German soldier raping his sister. He answered in his high-pitched voice, "I should try to interpose my own body." He was eventually rejected, not because of his arguments but because he was conspicuously medically unfit.[2]

Refusing military service was, as always in a war, considered un-patriotic, and conscientious objectors were subject to assault and imprison-ment, where they were abused and sometimes murdered with impunity. Duncan, with approval from the Foreign Office, tried to get to Paris to execute scenery for Copeau's *Pelléas et Mélisande*. At Dieppe, he was declared a "pacifist-anarchist" (he had probably tried to talk reasonably with military persons there). He was threatened with imprisonment in a concentration camp or immediate deportation. A British officer was particularly abusive and Duncan was harassed on the ship returning to England.

"Duncan took the line that he belonged to a tiny minority and that his views differed *in toto* from the majority on almost every subject. His opinions would never be attended to, and he would never fight for those of the majority, particularly as he believed it was always morally wrong to employ violence."[3] Duncan's moral courage was remarkable. He refused a War Artist commission on the same grounds, and because he would have had to wear the uniform of an army major.

On Maynard's advice, and aware of the grim fate of conscientious objectors, Duncan and Bunny moved to the country. To establish that they were really farm workers, they went to work on an abandoned farm belonging to Duncan's family, near Wissett, Suffolk. Duncan's father, a professional army officer, could not conceal his contempt for their evasion and referred to Bunny Garnett, in his hearing, as "your friend Garbage." Once Duncan and Bunny were settled in, Vanessa joined them, bringing her two lively boys who ran around naked, her cook, and a nursemaid. Maynard, Clive and others came to visit too (Number 10).

To identify their chickens, which they suspected were being stolen, the would-be farmers put blue dye on their white leghorns, making a patriotic

---

[2] The novelist Ronald Firbank, as fragile and precious as Lytton, was summoned again and again before the conscription tribunal until he finally threatened to sue them if they kept bothering him.

[3] *The Golden Echo, II,* by David Garnett, p. 123.

color scheme of red, white and blue, they thought. But this was considered a mockery by the local poultry farmers. The tribunal was not convinced that their innovations aided the war effort and they were required to find alternative work. Vanessa took charge and found them jobs with a farmer near Asheham (Virginia Woolf's house in Sussex). She then found a house for them all to live in: Charleston (Number 25).

It was a big house, "with a W.C., but the bath only has cold water," Vanessa wrote, with many bedrooms and with servants' quarters. There was a walled garden and a pond (Numbers 56 and 57). Later, studios and a kiln were added. In autumn 1916, Vanessa moved in with her two sons and Duncan and Bunny. Clive stayed in London but visited often. This was to be the country home of Vanessa, Clive and Duncan for the rest of their lives.[4] Maynard lived at 46 Gordon Square, which he had bought from the Bells, and where Clive continued to live too.[5] If the country dwellers wanted to be in London, they could always stay with Maynard or the Stracheys.

Duncan began full-time work as a farm helper. He also continued to do work of all kinds for Omega and to paint. "The Coffee Pot," c. 1916 (see book jacket back cover), is "one of the first pieces by an English artist in the early Cubist tradition to enter the [Metropolitan] Museum's collection... with its strong stripes of color and black handle [it] indicates the sensitive richness of color that was so natural to Grant."[6] He painted a portrait of his mother in 1917. A remarkable work, begun in 1914, is "The Kitchen" (Plate 35). Duncan reworked this painting and finally sent it to an exhibition held at the Omega in 1917. (Compare this with his earlier treatment of a kitchen— Number 34.) *The Times'* critic praised it, writing, "Here he seems to have remembered some Sienese painting, but he has produced something quite original with its own curious beauty both of design and execution." The woman on the left is a portrait of Vanessa Bell. Another notable work of this year is "Dancers— Homage to Matisse," 1917. Matisse's "Joie de Vivre," 1905-06, and "La Danse" (which had been shown in Roger Fry's Second Post-Impressionist Exhibition of 1912) were rings of female dancers. Duncan was inspired to create a painting of men dancing after seeing William Blake's "Oberon, Titania and Puck with Fairies Dancing." Richard Shone has observed, "The rhythmic possibilities of a circle of

---

[4]In 1980, two years after Duncan's death, the Charleston Trust was formed to buy and preserve the house.

[5]In 1925, Maynard bought Tilton, a farm which shared a boundary with Charleston.

[6]*Notable Acquisitions*, 1980-81, Metropolitan Museum of Art, p. 65.

dancers has been a feature all through Duncan's work."[7] For productions by Copeau, presented in New York in 1918, Duncan designed additional scenery for *Twelfth Night* and costumes for *Pelléas et Mélisande*. The costumes were cut and painted at Charleston. Maynard carried them to New York, where he had to go on a financial mission. Duncan also showed work in Zurich.

All this astonishing work was accomplished while he was working full time as a farm laborer; developing rheumatism, in a frigid house (coal was scarce), with only meager food rations, with sick children; sleeping with an ambitious young man who taunted him with his infidelity; and fending off the advances of a passionate middle-aged woman.[8]

Things were going badly in the triangle: Bunny had tried to seduce Vanessa, who rejected him, and Duncan was mad with jealousy because Bunny slept with Alix Sargent-Florence whenever he went up to London. Duncan made scenes, wept and even threatened to kill himself. He turned to Vanessa for sympathy and love, and began to sleep with her when Bunny was away. His crisis seemed to pass in the spring of 1918, when he finally became indifferent to Bunny's affairs.

Duncan's portrait of Vanessa (Number 54), done at this time, shows her calmly gazing into space, but with her hands in fists, tightly pressed together. She was pregnant. When she finally revealed her condition, Duncan told Maynard: "Clive took Nessa's news in the greatest good part." Indeed, Clive generously agreed to pretend to be the father. This saved Vanessa from the stigma of an intolerant society.

The Armistice came on 11 November 1918. Everybody was at the tremendous victory party at Montague Shearman's flat in the Adelphi. It was packed with people including Duncan, Bunny, Maynard, Ottoline, Clive, Mary and St. John Hutchinson, Lytton, Dora Carrington, Augustus John (in his British officer's uniform), the D.H. Lawrences, Mark Gertler, the Sitwell brothers, and the Huxley brothers. Even Serge Diaghilev, Leonide Massine and Lydia Lopokova arrived after a ballet performance. Everybody was there, except Vanessa. Eight months pregnant with Duncan's child, she had begun her *accouchement* in the country, at Charleston.

The peace, to Duncan's great relief, meant release from farm work. He began to paint again in London, using Roger's studio, but he continued to live at Charleston. Plans were made concerning the baby. Bunny stayed on at

---

[7] See another treatment of dancers in a circle, Number 50.

[8] The author asked Duncan Grant how he managed to cope with all this. "The farm work was terrible," was Duncan's only complaint.

Charleston to help with running the place, chopping wood, pumping water. Vanessa read a book to tell them what to do if there were no doctor present when the baby arrived. Duncan, Bunny and Maynard were in the house on Christmas Day, the first Christmas of peace, when Vanessa gave birth to a daughter. She remembered waking up, after the baby was born, and hearing farm workers singing Christmas carols.

Susannah, as Angelica was first called, was put on the kitchen scales in a shoe box and found to weigh 7½ pounds. The same day, Bunny wrote prophetically to Lytton: "I think of marrying it; when she is twenty I shall be 46—will it be scandalous?"

Bunny left Charleston in mid-January and returned unexpectedly some months later. Instead of a warm welcome, he found the young painter Edward Wolfe in his bed (Number 8). Now Bunny was the jealous party, threw a fit and wept, but Duncan was not moved. Bunny slept in the paddock that night.

CHAPTER 6

1919–1946

AFTER THE GREAT WAR, the Bloomsbury friends moved into the 1920's, middle-aged and successful. Maynard Keynes was an international figure. He had resigned, disillusioned, from his position with the Treasury at the Versailles Peace Conference. He returned to England and in August and September of 1919, in the first-floor bedroom at Charleston, wrote *The Economic Consequences of the Peace*, which was the basis of his subsequent fame. As befitted a brilliant economist, he made shrewd personal investments and became the wealthy member of the group of friends. He also looked after the capital of his friends, including Vanessa. He was in love with the ballerina Lydia Lopokova (Number 65), who was in love with him. They were married in 1925, and had perhaps the happiest relationship of any of the Bloomsbury group. Vanessa for many years resented Lydia and was disparaging of her.

Lytton Strachey became famous for *Eminent Victorians* and *Queen Victoria*. Before Lytton, biographies were sterile and adulatory, typically commissioned by the subject's family. Unlike these bowdlerized "official biographies," his examined the subjects with surgical ruthlessness. His later *Elizabeth and Essex* was more romantic, as he identified with the aging virgin queen in love with a virile young man.

After a struggle with Ottoline over the painter Henry Lamb (who was not interested in either of them), Lytton became enamored of Ralph Partridge, who was in love with the painter Dora Carrington, who of course worshipped Lytton. Partridge married Carrington and all three lived together in a friendly ménage at their country house, Ham Spray. This triangle continued until Lytton's death in 1932. Carrington did not wish to live without him and took her own life two months later. Ralph Partridge then married his mistress, Frances Marshall, whose sister was married to David "Bunny" Garnett.

Lytton's sister, Dorothy, who was married to the painter Simon Bussy, also formed a hopeless triangle. She had become the *traductrice accréditée* of the great French writer André Gide, who was also probably the most famous homosexual in France. After the war, with his young lover Marc Allegret, Gide had visited England and—in the best Bloomsbury tradition—Dorothy fell in love with him.

Virginia Woolf, despite bouts of madness, enjoyed the celebrity that came from her writing, and was tenderly cared for by Leonard Woolf. The Hogarth Press took up a lot of their time, and by 1921 they had published their own work and that of Katherine Mansfield, E.M. Forster, and T. S. Eliot, and began to publish Russian literature. In the years that followed they published work by Isherwood, Auden, Spender and others. Vanessa designed distinctive covers for her sister's books.

After recovering from his affair with Vanessa, Roger Fry lived happily with Helen Anrep, although they never married. He died in 1934. He was survived by five sisters and a daughter who were all concerned as to how his biography would be handled. Virginia consented to write it, but she made no mention of his love for Vanessa in the book. "She was still," David Gadd wrote, "to that extent the child of an eminent Victorian family."

Clive Bell led a busy social life internationally. As well as his residence in London and his room at Charleston, he had an apartment on the rue la Boétie in Paris, where he lived for weeks at a time, socializing with the Picassos, the André Derains, and many other artists, writers and composers. After a lunch chez Bell, Picasso did a drawing of Clive and his guests, including Cocteau, Satie and Olga Picasso. Clive was a famous host and often entertained with Maynard. He continued to write art criticism and published *Art* in 1919, *Since Cézanne* in 1922, and *On British Freedom* in 1923, expressing his concerns about censorship and sexual freedom. He was always concerned with improving the quality of life.

Duncan's studio in the back of 8 Fitzroy Street had been the studio of James McNeill Whistler, Augustus John and then Walter Sickert. (He kept it until it was destroyed by German bombs in 1940.) In February 1920, Duncan had his first one-man show, at the Carfax Gallery, and that year also exhibited at the Vildrac Gallery in Paris. In his review of the Carfax show, Clive Bell wrote: "At last we have in England a painter whom Europe may have to take seriously.... Duncan Grant is the best English painter alive.... I dare say Duncan Grant's most national characteristic is the ease with which he achieves beauty. To paint beautifully comes as naturally to him as to speak English does to me."[1]

---

[1] Reprinted in *Since Cézanne*, by Clive Bell, p. 105.

In 1923, Roger Fry's book *Duncan Grant* was published by the Hogarth Press. In it he wrote: "He pleases because the personality his work reveals is so spontaneous, so unconstrained, so entirely natural and unaffected. And these happy dispositions of his nature reveal themselves in his work—in his drawings by a singularly melodious and rhythmic line, in his painting by a corresponding fluency and elegance of handling. His naturalness gives him his singular charm of manner. But more than this, he has a peculiar happiness of disposition. A certain lyrical joyousness of mood predominates in his work. And this leads him to affect and enjoy what is beautiful in nature, and to express that delight in beauty in his work."

Over the next years he exhibited at the Independent Gallery in Grafton Street, until 1926 when the London Artists' Association (L.A.A.) was created by Maynard Keynes, with financial backing from Samuel Courtauld and others. Maynard's idea was to provide chosen artists with a small guaranteed income and management of their business affairs, plus sponsorship of their exhibitions. As well as Duncan, other artists supported by the L.A.A. were Vanessa, Roger Fry, Bernard Adeney, Keith Baynes, Frank Dobson, and F. J. Porter. Also in May 1926, Duncan was represented in the XVth Venice Biennale. Over the next six years, the L.A.A. showed his work, with others, in Berlin, New York (at the Marie Sterner Galleries), and Pittsburgh.

In 1931, to Maynard's disappointment and displeasure, Duncan, Vanessa and Keith Baynes left the L.A.A. to accept an offer to be represented by Thos. Agnew & Sons, one of the most prestigious galleries in London. As well as being a generous offer, this gave the painters more freedom to exhibit. Throughout the thirties their work appeared in many London galleries, as well as Agnew's, especially the Lefevre Gallery, where Duncan had a one-man show in 1934. Agnew's showed "Drawings by Duncan Grant" in 1933 and "From Gainsborough to Grant" in 1934, giving an indication of his established position in the British art pantheon.

He was in the XVIIIth Venice Biennale in 1932, and was represented in "Contemporary British Art" at the 1939 World's Fair in New York City. With another war looming, he was a member of the Advisory Committee of Artists' International Association for "Unity of Artists for Peace, Democracy and Cultural Development." In 1940, thirty-nine paintings were chosen for the XXII Venice Biennale, but not sent because of the war. They were shown instead in London at the Wallace Collection.

During these two decades, Duncan and Vanessa undertook many interior decoration projects. In 1921 they decorated rooms for Adrian and Karin Stephen; in 1922 finished work on Keynes' rooms at Cambridge; in 1924 executed a large mural for Raymond Mortimer in his flat; in 1926 decorated Clive Bell's flat at 50 Gordon Square; in 1926-28 executed decorations for Mr. and Mrs. Hutchinson in Regents Park; in 1927 decorated the "Garden Room" at Ethel Sands and Nan Hudson's Château d'Auppegard near Dieppe; and in 1929 they did their famous dining room for Lady Dorothy Wellesley, at her house, Penns-in-the-Rocks, finished in 1931.

Fabrics designed by Duncan, Vanessa and others for Allan Walton textiles were shown in 1931 at the Cooling Galleries, along with painted furniture, tiles and pottery. They designed fabrics for Walton until 1939. Duncan's "Apollo and Daphne" (Number 63) won a Medal of Merit at the 1937 Paris International Exhibition. In 1933, for the Lefèvre Galleries, they decorated and furnished a "Music Room."[2] They also designed rugs (Number 62). In 1934, at Harrods, they showed pottery designed for Foley china. In 1938, they carried out decorations for Ethel Sands' house in Chelsea.

Duncan loved theatre, opera and ballet (Numbers 64 and 69) and designed many costumes and décors during this period. He did a striking portrait, in the manner of Ingres' "Mlle. Rivière," of Lydia Lopokova, 1923 (Number 65). He did costumes for a Cochran review at Covent Garden in 1923, *Togo or the Noble Savage*, music by Milhaud, choreography by Massine, with Lopokova, Massine, Sokolova and Ninette de Valois (a distant cousin of Duncan's) among the dancers. The next year, he did scenery for *The Pleasure Garden* at the Regent Theatre, and he again dressed Lopokova, dancing with Rupert Doone, for a divertissement at the Coliseum. In 1925 he did costumes for Lopokova and Woizikowski for the ballet *The Postman* and the same year did sets and costumes for *The Son of Heaven*, by Lytton Strachey, at the Scala Theatre. In 1928, he did the scenery for George Ryland's production of Milton's *Comus*, the first given at the ADC Theatre in Cambridge and later at 46 Gordon Square, with Michael Redgrave and Lydia Lopokova. In 1932, he did costumes and scenery for two ballets, for the Camargo Society, *The Enchanted Grove*, choreographed by Rupert Doone and, from designs of Inigo Jones, the second act of *Swan Lake*.

Duncan's father, Bartle Grant, died in 1924. In his later life he had fallen into periods of depression and inactivity. He edited his great-grandmother's *The Receipt Book of Elizabeth Raper*, which was published after his death, with decorations by Duncan. Duncan admired his father, but in his eighties voiced a complaint common to sensitive sons: "...a very gifted man but I never got to know him intimately. I think he thought me rather a nuisance. Indeed, I was."

---

[2]This room was "recreated" in 1987 by Laura Ashley Ltd. to promote their line of fabrics based on designs by Duncan and Vanessa.

Duncan was, however, very close to his mother (Number 19). She was much admired by his friends as a tolerant and caring person. She is thought to be the model for Mrs. Flanders in Virginia Woolf's *Jacob's Room*. She was devoted to her two unmarried sisters, Daisy and Violet, concerned herself with her family's welfare and in particular looked after distressed female relations. She participated directly in Duncan's life by executing his designs for chair-seats, fire screens, and decorative panels in cross stitch and embroidery. She also worked designs for Roger Fry and Vanessa. In 1925, her work was included in "Modern Designs in Needlework," at the Independent Gallery, and examples are now in the Victoria and Albert Museum.

The big event of the thirties, which marked a downward turning point in Duncan's career, was a commission for three decorative panels for the Cunard Steamship Company's new super liner, the *Queen Mary* (Number 61). In 1936, after much work, Duncan's designs were rejected by the chairman of the line, Sir Percy Bates. A scandal ensued, with Kenneth Clark, Clive Bell, Raymond Mortimer and Samuel Courtauld raising indignant voices. A settlement was made, but Duncan's reputation was damaged and never recovered. Of course, he didn't care, but he was exhausted by the ruckus.

At the end of the First World War, Charleston was at first a summer home, but became a year-round base for Clive, Vanessa and Duncan, and their children, and many of their friends (Numbers 12 and 13). It was a good place for children, Vanessa felt, and there was also privacy, now lacking in London due to their celebrity. Old friends were welcome and came to stay and work, whether writing or painting (Numbers 17 and 18), and to play (Number 6).

Vanessa and Duncan and assorted friends made many trips abroad, often to Paris and St. Tropez (Number 11), but also Spain, Italy and Germany. In 1927, Duncan became ill while staying in the south of France, with his mother and Aunt Daisy, at Roland Penrose's villa "Les Mimosas," near Cassis. Vanessa, in London, was alarmed and set out at once with Angelica and her nurse Grace Higgens, who had become a part of the family and eventually was the housekeeper at Charleston. She found Duncan weak but recovering. While there, she fell in love with the area. They met a Colonel Teed, retired from the Bengal Lancers, who occupied himself with his vineyard, "Fontcreuse." They found him charming, and the Bells renovated a small house on his property, which they called "La Bergère." This was their vacation home, "Charleston in France," until 1939, when the Second World War began.

Duncan's appetite for romance was never sated. His lovers were tolerated by Vanessa because she had no choice. Around the time of Angelica's birth, Duncan told Vanessa he could no longer sleep with her; not because it didn't give him sexual pleasure, but because he could not bear the psychological tension this intimacy created. He wanted the security she represented, and she wanted him beside her, even if it meant a celibate life for herself. Frances Spalding wrote: "...in order to retain his love...she both tolerated his sexual adventures and defused the threat presented by his more permanent boy friends by absorbing them into their social life...."

Sometime after Bunny, and Teddy Wolfe, the Davidson brothers, Angus and Douglas (see rug designed by Douglas Davidson on the floor of Duncan's bedroom at Charleston—Number 26), took their turns as his favorite. In 1923, Duncan was seeing the young sculptor Stephen Tomlin (who would later marry Julia Strachey). In 1926, Angus Davidson, who had gone to work for the Woolfs at the Hogarth Press, accompanied Duncan and Vanessa on their trip to Venice. If these young friends happened to be painters, it was easier for Vanessa to establish contact with them. Franzi von Haas, an Austrian aristocrat and Peter Morris ("eyes of blue-green winter grass") were artists. Another painter friend of the late twenties was Robert Medley.

In 1929, the Bells' elder son Julian, now at Cambridge and elected an Apostle, wrote to his mother that he had been sleeping with a fellow undergraduate, Anthony Blunt.[3] Vanessa was overjoyed with the letter, for it proved to her that her favorite son trusted her enough to confide in her. As she no longer had any conjugal love in her life, she seemed to have made a particularly great emotional investment in Julian.

This same year, both boys were away and Vanessa decided to send Angelica to boarding school. For the first time in twenty-one years, she did not have children to look after and could return, as Virginia Woolf noted, "rather sadly to the life she would have liked best of all once, to be a painter on her own."

In about 1930, Vanessa recognized a particular threat from a young man of dubious background, George Bergen. He was said to have been born in a Jewish ghetto of Moscow before his father took him to Philadelphia. He was gauche, temperamental and brash, and was using portrait painting as a social entrée. His English was confused, and he spoke with an American accent. To Duncan, he was exotic. Duncan fell madly in love with George, who was the main interest in his life for years to come. He even considered living with him.

---

[3]Anthony Blunt, later head of the Courtauld Institute and Surveyor of the Queen's Pictures, and knighted by the Queen, confessed in 1964 that he had been a Soviet agent since his Cambridge days. His confession was kept secret and he maintained his prestigious posts for the next fifteen years. See Conspiracy of Silence, by Penrose and Freeman.

Vanessa went through a very bad period. George was aware that Vanessa didn't like him and was vindictive in return, also deliberately hurting Duncan. He once made advances to Vanessa's son Quentin in Duncan's presence. Duncan wrote of this relationship as being a "turmoil of love, anxiety, terror and sadness, and happiness...." He wrote to Bunny that he wanted both George and Vanessa, and that if she could see into his soul "she would see that everything is all right." Vanessa hung on.

On a visit to Rome, Duncan's attention shifted briefly to Jimmy Sheean, an American journalist, who loved to give cocktail parties for titled people. After a quarrel with him, Duncan turned to the charming Edward Sackville-West. While in Rome, Vanessa learned that Julian was considering marriage and she used her influence to convince him to give up the idea.

Back in London, for the opening of his show at the Cooling Galleries, Duncan had a great success, selling a lot of pictures and making new friends, particularly with the highly cultivated hostess Violet Hammersley, whose portrait he painted (Number 99 and compare with Number 20).

Vanessa was always contemptuous of fashionable society, which she avoided. Duncan, however, enjoyed high society *and* low society, including criminal fringes from the Tottenham Court Road who sometimes made their way into his studio. Vanessa would say, "Duncan's gone criminal again," after he met a Borstal boy. His generosity meant that a certain following of dependents developed, including a mentally disturbed man known as "Tut" (because he believed he was Tutankhamen reborn), to whom Duncan gave small sums of money.

Aside from her constant concern over Duncan, a series of setbacks were in store for Vanessa. In 1934, Roger Fry died, creating a great void in her life. The next year, her beloved son Julian announced he was going to take a job in China. Vanessa was very depressed by the news. At about this time, Vanessa told her seventeen-year-old daughter Angelica that "[her] father was not the man [she] had always believed him to be, but Duncan Grant." Angelica wrote that the reverberations she felt took many years to rise to the surface. Her mounting resentment at being the victim of this deception naturally created deep disturbances, which she has described in her autobiographical work, *Deceived with Kindness*. She felt that Vanessa had persuaded Duncan to "give her a child, prepared to take the responsibility on herself provided he remained close to her." Vanessa tried to make the case that Angelica had two fathers, but of course Angelica bitterly thought she had none. After this bombshell, Vanessa said no more, Duncan said nothing, and Angelica remained "closeted in dreams."

About this time, Vanessa painted a psychologically revealing portrait of

Duncan and his daughter, sitting at a table at Charleston (Number 74). There is an empty space between them. Duncan, oblivious of Angelica's presence except as a subject for his drawing, is contentedly absorbed in his work. Angelica sadly looks away from him and into the room, rather than out of the bright window behind her.

If Angelica was cut off from happiness by this revelation of her parentage, for Vanessa happiness ended with the death of Julian, in July, 1937, who had gone to Spain as a volunteer, where he worked as a stretcher-bearer. He was killed by shrapnel in an air attack. At the news of his death, Vanessa suffered a complete physical breakdown, a more severe form of what she had gone through at Roger's death. Duncan responded to Vanessa's prostration by staying close to her. After several months, they travelled to France, and upon returning to England, began to work together at the Euston Road School. She also occupied herself with collecting Julian's poems and other writings for publication. She turned to her son Quentin for help with this and also to Bunny Garnett, now a successful writer.

Suddenly Vanessa and Duncan found a common concern as parents. Working on fulfilling the prophecy he made at her birth, Bunny was flirting with Angelica. Vanessa and Duncan discussed the issue and decided an affair would be tolerable so long as it did not become serious. Bunny was twenty-six years older than Angelica, and married, with two small sons. Duncan made a great effort to discuss the situation with him. Bunny told Duncan not to interfere as it might affect Angelica's happiness. Duncan was outraged. Angelica capitulated to Bunny, and cut Vanessa out of her confidence. At this time, she did not know, apparently, of her lover's past sexual relationship with her father.

Bunny's wife was dying of cancer, and he took a room in Fitzroy Street to be able to meet secretly with Angelica. Ray Garnett, Bunny's wife, died in May 1940. Angelica and Bunny were married in the spring of 1942. Duncan and Vanessa were not invited to the wedding. In April 1943, Bunny and Angelica paid a conciliatory visit to Charleston, where Clive was jolly, Duncan tense and Vanessa "emitted an emotive power that bound together all the diverse emotions and personalities."[4]

War was declared on 3 September 1939. In this war, Quentin went to work on Maynard's farm. Vanessa and Duncan sublet their studios, packed up pictures and moved to Charleston. They bought chickens to keep for eggs and

---

[4]*Vanessa Bell*, by Frances Spalding, p. 323.

planted more vegetables in the garden. In 1940, Duncan was in a group show at the Lefevre Galleries and had a one-man show at the Calmann Gallery.

In this war, Duncan agreed to serve as a war artist, and spent May and June in Plymouth, where he confined himself to the naval barracks and naturally made many friends. Clive and Quentin enrolled in the Home Guard. In 1942, Duncan was elected to the Art Advisory Panel of the Council for the Encouragement of Music and the Arts. This cumbersome name gave way to the Arts Council of Great Britain.

Aunt Daisy prevailed upon her old friend Charles H. Reilly, a retired professor of architecture, to write to Dr. G. K. A. Bell, the Bishop of Chichester, proposing that Duncan decorate a Sussex church. The Bishop was delighted with the idea, as it fit with his ideals of art and the church coming together. Duncan went to Brighton to talk to the Bishop, and took advantage of the trip to also visit a sailor he had met at Plymouth. An architectural adviser was required for the church decoration scheme. Frederick Etchells, who had worked with Duncan on the Borough Polytechnic murals in 1911, turned up, now a successful architect.

The money was raised from Peter Jones, whose smart shop in Sloane Square had been designed by Charles Reilly. The next step was to get the approval of the local church council. The Bishop invited all the parishioners to a meeting in the village school, where opposition was so strong that Duncan decided to give up the project. The opposition had reared its ugly head in the form of the Hon. Mrs. Sandilands. Her objection turned out to be that she believed Vanessa's son Quentin to be a conscientious objector. When it was explained that he had been rejected from military service because he had tuberculosis, she dropped her objections, and the project could proceed.

Rather than painting on the wall, it was decided to paint on plaster boards which could then be set in the church. Maynard lent his barn as a studio and John Christie sent large-scale easels from the theatre at Glyndebourne. The work was a family affair, and even neighbors were used to pose, lend a lamp or help in other ways. Duncan's mother embroidered an altar cloth. In October 1943, the paintings were dedicated. The shock of delight that greets the viewer, according to Charles Reilly, is "like stepping out of foggy England into Italy."

After the church was finished, Vanessa and Duncan decorated the children's restaurant at Devonshire Hill School at Tottenham. The theme was Cinderella. Maynard, now Lord Keynes, made the opening speech. On Christmas Day, 1944, Maynard and Lydia gave a party for their employees and their families, which Duncan, Clive and Vanessa attended, along with

Grace Higgens' family. Lydia had accompanied Maynard on his wartime mission to America, and had brought back gifts for all forty guests, including 120 pairs of silk stockings. Duncan and Clive gave a performance of *Little Red Riding Hood*. Duncan played the wolf and terrified some of the little children.

PART II

1946–1978

Recollections

Because of the diverse conditions of humans, it happens that some acts are virtuous to some people, as appropriate and suitable to them, while the same acts are immoral for others, as inappropriate to them.—SAINT THOMAS AQUINAS, *Summa Theologica*

CHAPTER 7

Paul Roche

ON A PLEASANT SUMMER EVENING in 1946, on the north corner of Piccadilly Circus, Duncan Grant stood hesitantly waiting for a break in the heavy traffic. A sailor-boy with a bicycle was also trying to get across. When they had safely reached the south side of the Circus, the boy spoke to him: "That was a bit difficult, wasn't it?"

The boy looked to be about sixteen, with boisterous, curly blond hair and a sun-tanned face. Duncan was never one to shy away from an opportunity. After a brief exchange he asked the young sailor—he was wearing a sailor's blouse and dark trousers—if he liked pictures. Yes. The young man thought the "elderly gentleman" meant the cinema. So Duncan asked if he would like to come to look at some pictures. Then the young man realized the elderly gentleman meant paintings. Well, why not? They hoisted the bicycle into a taxi and set off for nearby Bedford Square. And so began a most unlikely and yet felicitous relationship, which was to develop and endure until Duncan's death thirty-two years later.

Duncan was financially secure, comfortable domestically with Vanessa Bell, surrounded by loving friends, and contentedly devoted to his work without concern for changing fashion. Still, in 1946, at the age of 61, he must have had some anxieties about the future of his romantic life, a critical part of his existence. Appreciated for his long-lasting friendships, and his ability to live in the immediate present, with no nostalgia for *temps perdu*, he was also known for his appetite for beautiful young men, an appetite as romantic as it was erotic, and integral to his creative process. Remarkably, throughout his life, he enjoyed a grand selection of male friends, conspicuous for their beauty and sometimes notable for their personal accomplishments. Many continued to be devoted to Duncan even after the sexual involvement was finished. Attractive men were as vital a source for Duncan's creative imagination as women were for Picasso's.

Still, any man, however poised and confidant, who wants romantic-sexual relationships with beautiful young persons of either sex, must dread aging. Besides its natural course, Duncan's life was filled with apocalyptic events. He had just lived through another world war, and seen his Fitzroy Street studio with his paintings turned to ashes from a German incendiary bomb. Other buildings where he had lived, worked and been entertained were also destroyed. Houses he and Vanessa had decorated were obliterated by the bombings, including the Woolfs' house in Tavistock Square. Only one wall of that house still stood after the bomb hit it, exposing to the open air the sitting room's mantelpiece with its decorations of garlands of fruit, which the rain quickly washed away. Duncan must have remembered the misfortunes of Piero della Francesca, who lost so many of his creations to wars and the demolition of buildings he had decorated.

Virginia Woolf, unable to bear any longer her descents into madness, had drowned herself in 1941. In 1942, to Duncan's great distress and anger, his daughter Angelica had married David Garnett, his own lover during the First World War. He had become a grandfather when their first child, Amaryllis Virginia, was born in 1943, soon followed by Henrietta Catherine Vanessa, and then the twins Nerissa and Frances. Maynard Keynes, Duncan's great friend and benefactor,[1] had died on Easter Sunday 1946. England's economy was in ruins. The Labor government was in power. Clive Bell spoke fancifully of emigrating to South Africa.

Sexual acts between men were still a dreadfully serious legal offense, and many distinguished careers had been ruined by police or blackmailers. John Gielgud had suffered police entrapment, Nöel Coward was alert to efforts of would-be blackmailers and Alan Turing, the brilliant cryptographer who had broken the German codes and directly helped to save Britain from defeat in the war, had been found dead as if a suicide. Many brilliant homosexual men had become Soviet agents: Anthony Blunt, Guy Burgess, Maclean and Philby, for examples; not so much because of an enthusiasm for communism but for a kind of revenge against terrible bigotry they had to suffer, against the criminal status a repressive society imposed on them.[2] Politically, Duncan was a true

---

[1] In 1937, Maynard provided a settled income for Duncan, who wrote him, "Dearest Maynard, I do not know how to thank you for what you are doing for me. . . . But honestly it is the greatest blessing that I need no longer worry about old age and decrepitude . . . quite apart from all the pleasure it will give me to have a little extra money now. . . . Much love, Duncan."

[2] In recent years, several excellent films have been made which deal with this subject, notably *Blade on the Feather*, 1980, the title taken from the Eton boating song, starring Donald Pleasance; *An Englishman Abroad*, 1984-85, starring Alan Bates; and *Another Country*, 1985, starring Rupert Everett and Colin Firth.

pacifist and his open life was a brave statement. When he refused to accept the honor of being named a Commander of the Order of the British Empire in 1950, it was his gesture of protest against the social order that in legal terms could also call him a criminal.

A new aesthetic, very far removed from Duncan's inspiration, prevailed in the art world. Ben Nicholson (b. 1894), Graham Sutherland (b. 1903) and Francis Bacon (b. 1909) were becoming the British painters with international recognition. Many people even supposed Duncan Grant was dead.

He faced all these enormous changes and pressures with equanimity and continued to paint with energy and originality. But there was an emotional void in his life, a gap left open by the departure of his last great favorite, George Bergen, who had gone to America well before the war had started. Duncan kept a painting by Bergen on the wall of his bedroom in Charleston, a view of the Spanish town of Pensacola.

So, in 1946, very much alive, with his sailor in a taxi, Duncan stopped in Shaftesbury Avenue to pick up a bottle of rum. Only a year after the war's end, it was still difficult to find anything palatable to drink, and the rum was very crude stuff, but the two began imbibing it as soon as they got inside a beautiful house in Bedford Square. This belonged to Edward le Bas (1904-66), a wealthy man of great cultivation, a graduate of Cambridge University, a discriminating collector and himself a painter, a Royal Academician and a member of the Artists International Association. His first one-artist show had been at the Lefevre Gallery in 1936. His style has been described as "safely within the Camden Town-Bloomsbury tradition, a high-keyed naturalism, fluent but unexceptional."[3]

Le Bas' collection was well known and included work by Matisse, Braque, Utrillo, Vuillard, Bonnard, and many contemporary British painters. He had purchased paintings by Duncan Grant and Vanessa Bell before he had ever met them. Duncan was always reluctant to sign his pictures, and the two men finally met when Edward asked him to sign a painting in his collection.

Duncan and Edward may have met through Patrick Nelson, a mutual boy-friend, a handsome young Jamaican who sometimes worked as an artist's model (Numbers 81 and 82). The two painters soon discovered they shared aesthetic sensibilities, and came to delight in each other's company and love of pleasure, which included drink. Edward became Duncan's great new post-war friend and confidant. Edward lent Duncan his house in Bedford Square, while he used a lovely studio in Glebe Place, in more fashionable Chelsea.

As for Vanessa, she was more and more jealous and suspicious of any new

---

[3]*Vanessa Bell*, by Frances Spalding, p. 333.

friend of Duncan's. On first meeting her, Edward said it was "touch and go." But Edward patiently wooed Vanessa for her friendship, reassuring her that he had no wish to steal Duncan away from her. Edward had his own romances, and he and Duncan were never lovers, which must have calmed her worst fears. Vanessa, who had begun to resist coming to London at all (in the past six years she had only spent two nights there), began to enjoy her visits, thanks to Edward's hospitality, his parties, and his invitations to Covent Garden. She also came to respect his deep love of painting, and although she found his work charming, it was too "feeble" for her taste. Today le Bas' work is represented in the Tate Gallery, and his portrait of Angelica, done in 1952, is in the collection of the Arts Council. Vanessa, Duncan and Edward became a social trio and would travel abroad, first to Dieppe, in 1946, and then further afield.

As they drank their crude rum, Duncan gave his sailor a tour of Edward's picture collection in Bedford Square: Walter Sickert, Harold Gilman, Charles Ginner, Mark Gertler, Augustus John, Gwen John, Paul Nash, Matthew Smith, Vanessa Bell, and, of course, Duncan Grant. With characteristic modesty, Duncan did not identify his own pictures. The young man knew nothing of painters or painting, although he knew the celebrity name Augustus John, and thought perhaps he had heard of Duncan Grant, who had reached the height of his fame in the 20's and 30's, but he could not be sure. Though out of sympathy with many of the pictures, there were a few that attracted him. He wondered if any of the pictures were by Duncan, as he chose four that he favored. "These are the ones I like best," he said, pointing them out. "Oh, I'm glad to hear it," said Duncan, "that one is by me and so is that."

Duncan's painting of a white handkerchief with colored borders, half spread out next to a glass cheese dish (Number 103 is possibly a study for this painting), hardly shattered the boy's ignorant eye, but as he sank down into a sofa he collapsed with laughter at Sickert's "Girl with the Black Brimmed Hat" smiling across at him. "She looks like a monkey," he said. The rum was beginning to have its effect. Duncan, by no means unmerry himself, then showed his drawing of a monkey, the witty and delicate cover design for Arthur Waley's *Monkey* (Number 92).

More rum and laughter and Duncan cautiously asked the young man to pose in the nude. There was no demur. The young man did not feel threatened and was, on the contrary, flattered and excited. He thought, "I am myself a person who adores beauty; for me the two things that make life worthwhile are beauty and freedom, so if he finds this object which is me beautiful, well, fine. Let him do this adoration. I don't mind. In fact, I think it's rather wonderful." That was his attitude. He also needed to be physically appreciated, and, of course, loved. "Some people will say this is narcissism. Fine, let it be narcissism. I am completely free," he told himself.

As for Duncan, he fell in love again. He parted from this young person with ardent hugs and a promise that he would return for a posing session the next day. Duncan was now dying to start to paint his portrait, and also full of anxieties that his Eros, known only as "Don," address unknown, would vanish as abruptly as he had appeared.

The young man had tumultuous emotions of his own. To begin with, he was not a sailor or a hustler, and he was not sixteen years old. He was a cleric in his mid-twenties, lately out of a seminary, a graduate of the Gregorian University in Rome and currently attached to St. Mary's Roman Catholic Church, Cadogan Gardens, Chelsea, to which he now pedalled home. His name was Paul Roche, known as Don to his family and friends. His meeting with Duncan would resolve the religious dilemmas that had troubled him since his adolescence.

Paul's father, like Duncan's, had been in the Army, in this case the Royal Engineers, stationed in India. Like Duncan, Paul as a child went back and forth from India to England. They had had a splendid house in Poona, called Eagle's Nest, which had been built by the Sassoon family. Paul's mother died suddenly of smallpox when he was about eight or nine. His father then took leave and took his three children back to England. The two boys were sent to Ushaw, the old Catholic public school near Durham. It was there Paul became very ill, at about age fourteen, with what he described as "a mysterious disease of 'scruples,'" which lasted in virulent form for nearly five years.

After Ushaw he attended day school at Ealing Priory School, where he was considered such bright material that it was decided to send him to the English College in Rome. He was still suffering from various religious maladies. "The one thing you must not do at the age of eighteen is to take philosophy seriously, and I took it seriously," he has said. He recovered from philosophic madness by wandering around in Europe on his bicycle, and it was on return from one of these rambles that he encountered Duncan Grant in Piccadilly Circus.

The very next day, as promised, Paul returned to Bedford Square, shed his uniform, and was put to posing. Although it was still summer, Duncan lit the gas fire to keep his naked subject warm. The first painting of Paul, lying on a beautiful rug in Edward's drawing room (Number 85), caused Duncan enormous difficulty because the light wasn't good. Duncan's stamina to work on it for hours and hours was matched by Paul's ability to pose, with only little breaks every twenty minutes or so. Duncan found a beautiful person to look at to his heart's content. Paul found an admirer whose attention to him was tireless and whose love would help him to spiritual and intellectual independence and maturity.

Most of his adult life, Duncan had Vanessa's unspoken but obvious jealousy to contend with, but early on, since the move to Charleston, a pattern of toleration was established. They travelled abroad *en ménage*, worked together often side by side, and spent half of each week together in the country. His double life operated relatively smoothly. Paul's situation, however, was different. Their chance meeting was to force issues which would completely alter his life. Both he and Duncan, however, time would prove, would never grow too old to enjoy themselves, with intellectual, spiritual, childlike and sensual delights.

As the pattern of their relationship developed, Paul continued to offer neither resistance nor encouragement to Duncan. Duncan was frightened at the thought that Paul might vanish and never come again. "Will you continue to let me love you? How I wish we could be friends. May I love you?" he would ask. "Yes," was the answer. Paul was troubled that one day he would have to say, "From now onwards, Duncan, you mustn't think of my body, but love me." For the present, however, he let it pass and refused to worry about it.

There were plenty of other things to worry about. He hated to deceive Duncan about his occupation and identity but couldn't face telling him. He clung to the present. "How wonderfully good and kind and delicate is this old man," he thought. "He goes out of his way to avoid making awkward inquiries and yet he must want to know everything about me. Oh, how I wish I could tell him."

Duncan was afraid of displeasing Paul and frightening him away. "Why does he come at all?" was Duncan's question to himself, and how to keep him from being bored was a concern, however needless. For several weeks, one of the first things Paul used to hear in the preliminary quarter of an hour of Duncan's raptures at meeting was: "I knew you would come, I knew you wouldn't let me down," followed by, "Oh, Don, promise me that you will never go away suddenly, you must give me warning." Paul promised himself that he would never grieve the old man by suddenly disappearing. That had been his vague plan at first, but now he saw he would never be able to bring himself to do it. He knew he came partly for selfish and conceited reasons. He liked being admired. He liked being drawn and painted, and he had by now some sense of Duncan's stature as an artist. He liked money being spent on him, and he liked the novelty and adventure of the whole affair.

Duncan's habit of coming to London by train for three or four days in mid-week was already established, but now Paul was part of it. Paul, however, had many risks involved in meeting Duncan. He had the problem of getting away from his duties at St. Mary's, and ran the risk of being recognized, out of his clerical clothes, by parishioners. He continued to deceive Duncan into thinking he was a sailor in the Royal Navy, all the more so because Duncan liked to draw and paint him in uniform (see photo by Duncan Grant, Number 15). He liked to meet Duncan's train in Victoria Station, under the clock at 11:00 a.m. On arrival, Duncan would go down to the barber shop to be shaved. Paul would wait for him and then they would go to drink brown ales in the station pub. Duncan would gaze at Paul for minutes on end, and they would talk until the last possible moment when Paul would have to hurry back to St. Mary's to be in time for lunch.

The first painting of Paul, on Edward le Bas' rug, took about six days of sittings. That established the pattern of posing. Duncan was happy with the new relationship, and anxious to strengthen it. He rented a room from his cousin Marjorie Strachey (Number 36), in her flat in Bloomsbury, at No. 1 Taviton Street and suggested to Paul, "Why don't you live in this room? Then you'll be here when I come up to London." Paul accepted with pleasure. It became his room.

Marjorie, who taught at a school in Sussex but lived in London, had no trouble in accepting Paul. She shared her little kitchen and bathroom with him for the next eight years. Paul remembers their relationship with pleasure and remembers her too as a most undomestic person. On one occasion she heated a tin of spaghetti which exploded, creating a beautiful red design across the ceiling where it remained over the years.

She was constantly forgetting pans on the stove. When a pan began to burn, pouring fumes and smoke from the kitchen, instead of going and removing the pan she would telephone the fire brigade. Paul went every day to the YMCA·on Great Russell Street for exercise and a shower, and on two or three occasions returned to find Taviton Street filled with fire engines and fire hoses. He learned to say, "Well, Marjorie's left another saucepan on the stove."

Duncan always arrived in London carrying a small portmanteau, like a doctor's bag. Although indifference to fashion was a Bloomsbury tradition, Duncan was the most neglectful of them all. He would wear anything at hand and was most typically in need of braces or a belt to hold up his pants. However, looking forward to a social activity in London, he carried in the satchel, along with his paint brushes and paint, a clean shirt and an evening dress suit.

On top of the case he would have an enormous bunch of flowers from his garden at Charleston, oriental poppies, irises, whatever was blooming.

Duncan seldom painted flowers in London, as he was busy with nudes and portraits. The flowers were for his mother or his aunts. Paul felt some resentment that they were never brought for him, and sometimes he would say, "Let's keep them."

The first thing Duncan would do on arrival was to telephone Edward, a conversation Paul says never varied:

"Edward, I am here, I'm here in London. Don is here. Will you. . . . We think that you should come to dinner."

Edward: "No, I think you had better come to dinner to me."

Duncan: "Well, but I think that's not fair, you've given us so many dinners."

Edward: "Never mind, I've a capon which I bought this morning, it's all ready. Come over tonight."

Once in a rare while, they would give Edward dinner, never in a restaurant, but prepared in Marjorie's kitchen in Taviton Street. Paul cooked while Duncan, a very good cook himself, asked questions and gave advice. Usually, however, Paul and Duncan took the bus down the King's Road to Edward's studio in Glebe Place. These dinners were usually just for the three of them, but sometimes they were joined by Eardley Knollys, the art dealer who had become a painter.

They would be given drinks immediately. Edward would have fixed a superb dinner, combining his culinary skills with delicacies ordered from Fortnum & Mason: shrimps, oysters and perhaps a pheasant with sauce of wild mushrooms, or red mullet stuffed with sweet basil. And there was always a superb wine. Edward showed his latest paintings and the drink continued to flow. By two in the morning the rows began. The two painters achieved a zenith of mutual insult and then subsided. By then a taxi had been called, to which Duncan happily staggered on Don's arm, genuflecting on the pavement before flopping onto the taxi's floor. Thus would the two of them return home to Taviton Street.

Occasionally Duncan would take Paul to a film, or the opera. A series of standard fare was being given at the Cambridge Theatre in Cambridge Circus, so Paul's first operas were *Tosca*, *La Bohème*, and the like. It was at the opera that Duncan and Paul ran into Clive Bell, to Duncan's consternation. Clive delightedly gossiped to Frances Partridge: ". . . Perhaps you don't know that a handsome young able-bodied seaman is often to be seen [with Duncan at Taviton Street] in full uniform. I have seen him myself—with Duncan—at a performance of *Carmen,* and I'm bound to say he is extremely able-bodied. Please use utmost discretion."[+]

But whatever the diversions, Duncan was most of all anxious to get back to his easel. He could spend the entire day drawing and painting, working until late at night. Even after the theatre, Duncan would want to paint. Paul mixed blue and red colored light bulbs for Duncan, trying to get a satisfactory light to work under at night.

Duncan gave the *coup de grâce* to Paul's scruples and a period ensued in which he simply threw over religion altogether. "Duncan was a sort of tonic for me," Paul has said, and he experienced new intellectual excitement. He had previously read mostly theology and philosophy, neglecting poetry and fiction. Duncan, his paternal instincts aroused, as they had not been with his daughter, undertook to expand and advance Paul's education. Although he modestly considered himself uneducated, intimidated perhaps by the formidably critical intellectuals who were his intimate friends, Duncan was a great reader. He directed Paul's reading, his appreciation of music, and to train his eye, took him on his rounds to museums and private galleries, to Agnew's, Lefevre, and Adams. Brothers. Most perceptively, Duncan encouraged Paul to write, saying "Don, you're a poet. Why aren't you writing?" thereby helping him to realize his true vocation.

[+]*Vanessa Bell,* by Frances Spalding, p. 335.

CHAPTER 8

1946-1952

DUNCAN'S OBSESSION with Paul created great difficulties, as Vanessa always feared any new person was a threat to their relationship. All new friends had to be vetted by her. She coped with many of Duncan's affairs by becoming friendly with each lover in his turn and, trusting to the transitory nature of these affairs, waited them out. Even though some of these lasted for years, Vanessa outlasted all of them but the one with Paul.

Paul at first didn't even know of Vanessa's existence, never mind her place in Duncan's life. Early on in their relationship, Duncan would complain: "Oh, if only certain people would understand. Certain people can't see how perfect this is or how beautiful this is. Certain people...." Later Paul would realize that "certain people" meant Vanessa. He was to be baffled that a woman old enough to be his grandmother could be jealous of him—but eventually he would become jealous in his own way of Vanessa's hold on Duncan.

Even after he had met Vanessa, Paul made no special efforts to charm her, not realizing her central role in Duncan's life. Vanessa then did make an effort to become acquainted with him. Paul posed for her and Duncan at Taviton Street on several occasions. She was kind and friendly, but ill at ease. She clearly was pained to see the domestic bliss of the *garçonnière* and the two men's mutual delight in their arrangements.

Duncan repeatedly asked Paul to live with them at Charleston, which would have meant being folded into the environment controlled by Vanessa. Paul, with mixed feelings as he came to understand the situation, felt he must decline. In fact, he rarely visited Charleston while Vanessa was alive. Vanessa's sense of isolation, which had grown worse since the death of her son Julian, intensified, as she felt cut off from Duncan's deepest, most intimate feelings. Her unhappiness was keenly felt by Duncan, who was troubled by the sense of guilt she provoked in him.

Still, Vanessa, now in her late sixties, was enjoying a more sociable existence than she had led during the war. She enjoyed her granddaughters, a link with Duncan as they were his progeny, too. She had gone, in 1946, with Duncan and Edward to war-damaged Dieppe, where they set up studios in some empty rooms of one of the few hotels still in operation.

Vanessa and Duncan met their old patrons Ethel Sands and Nan Hudson, who took them to their Château d'Auppegard, where twenty years earlier Duncan and Vanessa had painted decorations in the loggia. The château, so exquisitely restored in the late 1920's, had been damaged by a bomb, and looted and vandalized by German soldiers, who had despoiled the Bell/Grant designs. The elegant ladies, now unable to afford repairs to the château, lived in a few undamaged rooms amidst the wreckage. Duncan and Vanessa spent an afternoon there, repairing their work.

As Britain began the struggle to recover from the devastation of the war, Vanessa and Duncan were forgotten artists. They were outside the consideration of a new generation of critics and tastemakers, who viewed with distaste any art which did not reflect the grim reality of life in the post-war period. Horrors and deprivations were acceptable themes politically—there must be no nostalgia for the irresponsible 1930's which led to the catastrophe of the war. "Serious" artists were now expected to deny any impulse of decorative frivolity or fun. They were supposed to reflect the austerity of the times, and to work in rarified abstraction.

As Duncan and Vanessa had never depended on fashion for inspiration, appreciation or income (they had themselves been trend setters for more than two decades), they continued to work according to their own aesthetic instincts. Not until the 1960's would figurative design work its way back into the category of fine art, a development sparked in part by David Hockney's international success.

Vanessa and Duncan worked on without concern for their diminished reputations. In May 1946, Miller's Gallery in Lewes presented an Omega show, and the possibility of reviving the Workshops was brought up, but the idea was abandoned. The two painters had rejoined the London Group and there were generally examples of their paintings on view at the Lefevre Gallery. Queen Elizabeth, the wife of King George VI, a discriminating collector, had purchased Duncan's "St. Paul's Cathedral," 1939. After the war, she commissioned him to do another portrait of the cathedral as, surrounded by rubble and the devastation of the German bombings, it survived to become a symbol of Britain's victory.

Duncan loved gardening, so a notable event at Charleston in 1947 was the flowering for the first time of the magnolia grandiflora, planted in front of the house some twenty years before. That year Angelica took up painting, and Vanessa and Duncan were concerned to help her further her career. Quentin's first book, *On Human Finery,* was published. In the autumn, Duncan, Vanessa and Edward went off to Paris, where they saw old friends and mingled with fellow artists, including Vanessa's old admirer, André Dunoyer de Segonzac, and Georges Duhuit and his wife, the daughter of Matisse.

Duncan's mother was ailing and had been to see a famous gynecologist, Alex Roche, Paul's cousin. In consultation with Dr. Roche, she had decided to "go as I am" rather than undergo surgery. Ethel Grant died sometime after Christmas 1947. She and Duncan had enjoyed a remarkable relationship. She had executed many of his designs in needlework. He had been a devoted son, taking her on many of his trips abroad. Every week until her death he had made the time-consuming trip by underground to Twickenham, to deliver flowers and have tea. In her final illness he was with her every day. After Ethel's death, he continued to visit and care for her sister Violet.

In autumn of 1948, Duncan, Edward and Vanessa went on a painting holiday to Lucca and Venice. Angelica, now disillusioned with her marriage to Bunny Garnett, was with her parents, happy to be away from the drudgery of motherhood and housekeeping. They stayed at the Pensione Seguso on the Zattere and spent most of their time painting. Vanessa was pleased to be with Angelica and, although Edward was teased for exhibiting at the Royal Academy, the mood was pleasant and relaxed, with many ices and much coffee and grappa consumed at Florian's.

Paul was not pleased to be cut out of Duncan's holidays but made up for it by going on a holiday of his own, to Brussels and then to Sicily. In Venice, Duncan concealed the distress he felt from Paul's letters (Paul told him of sexual adventures with women). But back in England, Duncan was once again faced with two powerful rivals for his love and attention. In December 1948, Duncan, who hated confrontations, sat down in the middle of the night to write a letter to Vanessa, to try to explain his mixed emotions.

Noting that the wind was howling outside the house, he wrote that it was so difficult to talk with her about things of mutual concern. He says he cannot bear to think that she is unhappy because of him. It makes him feel guilty. He thinks she does not understand at all how much he loves her and Angelica. He says that she laughs at him when he tries to tell her how much he admires her work as a painter. Then he gets to the reason for the letter, which is to say that it is difficult to tell her of his feelings for Paul. He thinks she is hard on Paul.

He says he loves him, but surely one can love a good many people. He explains how happy Paul makes him, and how Paul encourages him to work. He ends by saying that because Paul helps him, he is helping Vanessa too. It must have been a difficult letter[1] to write, and for all its honesty, it cannot have given Vanessa any comfort.

Again in 1949, Vanessa and Duncan were in Lucca in September. Paul also continued his separate European holidays every summer, "always with great moans and groans from Duncan, and I'd say, 'Well, Duncan, why don't you come with me?'" Paul in fact pleaded with Duncan to accompany him, but Duncan was afraid of Vanessa's reaction, which undoubtedly would have been silent reproach and deep misery. Paul did not have a holiday with Duncan until they went to Turkey, in 1973.[2]

In 1950, Duncan and Vanessa toured France by car, with a visit to Venice. That year, he became a member of the Society of Mural Painters, and with Vanessa was invited to participate in the "60 Paintings for '51" exhibit. This was the first show sponsored by the Arts Council of Great Britain and was part of the 1951 Festival of Britain. The Arts Council hoped to stimulate artists by requiring that all paintings in the show be at least 45" × 60". Canvas and paints were given to the sixty artists free of charge. In the depressed state of England's economy, the cost of paint and canvas was significant for many of the artists. The Arts Council hoped to find "public patrons" who would purchase the work shown. The goal was to rekindle the art market.

Duncan's contribution was "The Arrival of the Italian Comedy." The exhibition and its catalogue were amazingly dreary. Sir Colin Anderson, who had helped to select the artists for the show, made damning remarks on most of the works shown and called Duncan's and Vanessa's contributions "pathetic." These paintings did not find buyers and were put away in the attic at Charleston.

Anne Olivier Popham was an art historian who sat occasionally for Duncan and Vanessa when she visited Charleston. She and Quentin were married in February 1952. Quentin accepted a teaching post at King's College, Newcastle, and so that autumn Vanessa and Duncan took over Olivier's flat in 26a Canonbury Square, in Islington, then an extremely *déclassé* area. Olivier and Quentin's son Julian was born in October 1952, and Vanessa was delighted to have another grandchild.

---

[1] Letter from D. Grant to V. Bell, 6 December 1948, Charleston Papers, King's College, Cambridge.

[2] See *With Duncan Grant in Southern Turkey*, by Paul Roche.

The painting holiday that year was in Perugia and Lucca, and Duncan began sending work to the Royal West of England Academy at Bristol, becoming a member there in 1953.

The Royal Academy represented, to Duncan and his colleagues, the worst in British art. Since they had formed the London Group in 1914, specifically to oppose the Royal Academy's position as arbiter of art in Britain, there was enmity between the two groups. (Also, as a student, Duncan had been rejected by the Royal Academy, which hurt him deeply.) By the 1950's, however, the Royal Academy wished to include Duncan at its functions. He now snubbed them.

Paul encouraged Duncan to forgive and forget, saying, "Oh, Duncan, it's silly to go on having this quarrel. They've passed the phase of having only bad pictures." With further jollying encouragement from Royal Academician Edward le Bas, Duncan finally accepted an invitation to a party after a dinner for the Royal Family, to be held in the Royal Academy galleries.

Vanessa was also invited, but declined. She had always hated these high-society functions, and now in her seventies wrote, "I simply couldn't face it." Edward le Bas invited them to dine at Claridges and she knew his sister would be serving as his companion, "in her grand Molyneux" gown. Vanessa's indifference to fashion was by choice, but on such occasions her femininity was sensitized and she had no intention of appearing at a disadvantage. "One has to feel a good deal stronger than I did to go to such things," she wrote. Her sister Virginia shared this "dress complex" and has described how she declined many invitations from Lady Colefax of Argyll House because of it: "I hate being badly dressed; but I hate buying clothes."[3]

Duncan capitulated and attended the Royal Academy gala. Duncan loved parties, and he very much enjoyed himself, talking with his admirer and patron Queen Elizabeth. As they conversed, however, he had to use one hand to hold up his trousers, for as usual he had neglected to wear braces or a belt. In the midst of this *tête-à-tête*, Augustus John, in flamboyant splendor, bore down on the Queen and simply cut Duncan out, leaving him to retreat, adjusting his pants.

Soon after the Arts Council exhibition, Duncan was to receive a major commission (Vanessa was on the deciding jury), to decorate the Russell Chantry, dedicated to St. Blaise, in Lincoln Cathedral. Lincoln was once the center of the wool trade and Duncan created two large murals, "The Good Shepherd Ministers to His Flock" and "The Wool Staple in Medieval

---

[3]*Moments of Being*, "Am I a Snob," pp. 188-9, by Virginia Woolf.

Lincoln." Duncan did many studies of sheep, an easy subject for him in Sussex where the downs were covered with grazing animals. Of course he used Paul as his model for the Young Christ, whom he depicted as a beardless shepherd as seen in the earliest Christian iconography, the catacomb Christ, the Mercurial Christ, the Christ cloned from Hermes. Photos taken at the time show a mock-up of one of the murals (Numbers 100 and 101).[4] Duncan's historically valid but rather human representation of Jesus did not please everyone. The chapel was closed to the public as a result, only to be opened on request.

Biographers and historians were now beginning to invade the Blooms-buryites' privacy. Leonard Woolf's four volumes of memoirs were beginning to appear. Roy Harrod was working on his biography of Maynard Keynes, which would completely ignore Maynard's sexual relationship with Duncan. Noël Annan was doing a study of Leslie Stephen, Aileen Pippett disturbed them with her biography of Virginia Woolf, and Bunny Garnett was at work on the second volume of his autobiography, *The Flowers of the Forest*, for which work Vanessa refused him permission to quote from one of her letters.

At the same time, old animosities were rekindled as the Omega Workshops entered into art history via John Rothenstein's *Modern English Painters*, in which the quarrel with Wyndham Lewis is exaggerated into a sinister conspiracy. Rothenstein accused the Bloomsbury friends of promoting each other and of working together as an artistic cabal to ruin the careers of talented young painters and writers who did not follow their "party line." If these unnamed persons possessed "gifts of an order to provoke rivalry, then so much the worse for the artists. And bad it *was*, for there was nothing in the way of slander and intrigue to which certain of the 'Bloomsburys' were not willing to descend. I rarely knew hatreds pursued with so much malevolence over so many years; against them neither age nor misfortune offer the slightest protection."[5] Rothenstein's generalities were presented without substantiation. Even easy-going Duncan was so appalled by this slander that he wrote to Rothenstein, and although others too have asked Rothenstein to justify his charges, he has never done so.[6]

Lewis persistently attacked Bloomsbury in his writings, and Rothenstein was obviously influenced by these. He may have shared some of Lewis' social attitudes, and personally disliked Bloomsbury, the group often being per-

---

[4]Note on the left of the photograph a set-up for a still life, with a spotted scarf. This was the scarf used in "Poppies," c. 1955. See Number 102.

[5]*Modern English Painters*, by John Rothenstein, p. 14-15.

[6]Rothenstein's work is used as basic source material by scholars who thus perpetuate the myth, as, for example, in Jeffrey Meyers' *The Enemy. A Biography of Wyndham Lewis*.

ceived as being anti-Semitic, anti-Catholic, anti-Christian, anti-decent-middle-class Victorian values, and so on. Another ingredient in Rothenstein's hostility might have been that in the 1910's Roger Fry had preempted William Rothenstein's place as the most influential avant-garde critic-impresario in England.[7]

Whatever the basis for personal antipathy, it may have come to a head when John Rothenstein came to Charleston for lunch and, airing his views on art, remarked that Titian could not draw. At that point, Vanessa, outraged at this assertion, had made her detestation of him abundantly clear with a contemptuous stare. Frances Spalding writes that Rothenstein "cowered visibly and momentarily lost his social aplomb." His revenge was to lose no opportunity to denigrate both Duncan and Vanessa's work. "What a little worm he is," was Vanessa's opinion. Paul Roche said that Rothenstein was the only person he ever heard Duncan being nasty about, saying, "Don't mention that beetle, that thing."

---

[7]*Augustus John*, by Michael Holroyd, pp. 371-372.

CHAPTER 9

1952-1961

PAUL'S LIFE at Taviton Street continued to include posing for Duncan, for photography as well as sketches and paintings. Duncan loved photographs and cut them out of newspapers and other sources. The painting of basketball players (Number 86) is based on a Press-Sports photo. He liked to photograph his models (Numbers 17, and 18). He photographed Paul (Numbers 15 and 16), also commissioning a professional "physique" photographer to take pictures of him (Number 14). These photographs were references for some of Duncan's erotic drawings and paintings. Then as now, nudity was suspect and erotic photography was illegal, so utmost discretion was essential.[1]

A photo of Paul in the bath was the basis for several paintings, one of them purchased by Carlos Peacock.[2] John Lehmann and Benjamin Britten bought pictures of Paul in his sailor suit. Duncan also loved costumes and fabrics, and enjoyed searching for interesting examples when travelling, amassing a museum quality collection. Paul often dressed up from this wardrobe, in Chinese robes, and sometimes in grandfather Grant's kilts. Duncan took childlike delight in theatricals and dressing up, too, and especially loved headgear, hats and turbans of all kinds (Numbers 6, 7, 28 and 46).

The double set of double lives created mounting strain on everyone. By now Paul felt he should be living at Charleston, and Duncan wanted to take him there, whether Vanessa liked it or not. He would plead, "Why don't you come and live at Charleston?" Paul really wanted to go, but he felt it would make unbearable tension. And, he supposed, he might decide to marry in the future. Duncan had told Paul right from the beginning that he considered him

---

[1]Clive Bell had a taste for erotica and amassed a considerable collection of photographs, strictly heterosexual in subject matter, purchased during his trips to North Africa.

[2]Writer and art historian, who wrote a volume on Constable.

the son he always wanted. He also often told Paul "You must have a child." This was in the abstract, however. Paul thinks Duncan entertained the vague idea that he would just bicycle out into the Italian countryside, impregnate a nice healthy peasant girl and bring a baby boy home to Duncan.

Paul also began to have misgivings about what he saw as Duncan's sacrifice to Vanessa, of spending half his time secluded in the country with this quietly domineering old lady. In Duncan's 1942 portrait of her she is magisterial, sitting in a throne-like chair (Number 55). Duncan was by nature a sociable creature, with a wide range of friends, including important patrons and supporters, Queen Elizabeth and Sir Kenneth Clark, for examples. He was a darling of English aristocratic society. As Vanessa became more and more withdrawn, and as he had to spend so much time with her, his range of contacts necessarily diminished. Paul suggests that Vanessa's sequestration of Duncan kept him from becoming an international figure.

But despite Duncan's passionate love for Paul, his sense of loyalty to Vanessa was unshakable. She was above all a constant in his life, the person he could trust completely and whose tolerance had held against all tests, including sexual rejection. His experiences with a parade of men had shown him nothing to come near it, and although Paul would prove himself another constant, experience of such absolute trust lay in the future. In 1952 Vanessa's power held and something had to give.

Paul had long since broken from the church and was flourishing in his new life. Taking Duncan's advice, he had begun to write. *The Rat and the Convent Dove and Other Tales and Fables*, was published in 1952. It was followed in 1954 by *O Pale Galilean*, with a cover designed by Duncan (Number 96), who had also suggested the title from a line in a poem by Swinburne. Paul began to gain some notice as other than Duncan's young friend. He appeared on John Lehmann's program on the BBC and met Stephen Spender. A short-lived friendship developed, cut off by Paul's failure to respond to Stephen's ardent letters. When Paul complained of these, Duncan told him, "But you have to remember, Stephen is a very great booby."

While continuing his relationship with Duncan, Paul began to have girl friends. This bothered Duncan considerably, although it was not something outside his experience. Duncan's lovers were often heterosexual, as Paul was. A crisis of sorts developed when Paul suddenly found he had made two girls pregnant, almost simultaneously. Paul decided that he would marry Clarissa, an American. She had made a great impression on him by saying he certainly didn't need to think he had to marry her just because she was pregnant. His poem "Letter to a Young Girl Contemplating Marriage to a Poet" was addressed to her as a kind of warning disclaimer.

Paul's first child was a boy, Tobit, whom Duncan considered his first "grandson" (Number 23), and Clarissa's first child Pandora was born soon after. Clarissa and Paul would have three more children: Martin, Vanessa and Cordelia (Number 21). This family became a source of joy to Duncan (Numbers 22) and helped create the happy ambiance at Charleston after Vanessa's death. Quentin Bell and his family, when at Charleston, always behaved "correctly" toward the Roches. Angelica, on the other hand, could scarcely bear them and she and Clarissa were to clash.

Duncan was upset when Paul told him he intended to marry. But he was really more shattered by the news that the couple would leave England. His first letters, written in anger, pursued Paul to Michigan. As Paul wrote back to him, he came to accept the situation. They continued to correspond during the eight years Paul lived in America, Duncan writing almost every week.[3]

The coronation of Queen Elizabeth II was in June, 1952. Duncan and Vanessa watched the ceremonies on Edward le Bas' television set, lunching on plovers' eggs and raising many glasses of champagne to the new Queen's health. That summer Quentin began what would become a habit of bringing his family to Charleston for his long summer vacations. Clive as always shared Charleston with Vanessa and Duncan. Now he found himself once again in the house with a small child, but this time as a grandfather and without servants to look after the baby. In autumn the annual painting holiday was in Auxerre. That same year there was an exhibition of past members of the London Artists Association, at the Ferens Art Gallery in Hull.

Vanessa and Duncan travelled together to Newcastle in May 1953, to visit Quentin and Olivier and to see Vanessa's grandson, Julian. The visit was memorable for Vanessa's borrowing the car to shop in town, but returning by bus, forgetting where she had parked. Vanessa and Duncan travelled on to visit friends in Edinburgh, where Duncan was disappointed to see so few kilts.

In 1954, Duncan accepted an invitation to visit Deborah Mitford, the Duchess of Devonshire, in Ireland. His painting of the Cavendish house there, Lismore Castle, Waterford (Number 79), now hangs in the Duchess' bedroom in Chatsworth House, Derbyshire. He also painted her portrait (Number 80).

Vanessa went alone to Roquebrune to visit the Bussys, and went on with Dorothy Bussy to Antibes and Venice, to see the Matisse chapel. She was

---

[3]When he returned to England in 1961, Paul returned these letters to Duncan, who put them in a tin box, together with Paul's letters to him. After his death, although Paul's letters remained, Duncan's letters were missing from the box, and their fate is unknown. Another mysterious question is the whereabouts of the bust of Paul, which Duncan commissioned from Keith Godwin.

horrified that Matisse, with no Christian beliefs, had accepted the commission. This seems odd considering the fact that she and Duncan both decorated churches. On returning to Paris, she heard the sad news of the death of Simon Bussy, Duncan's early mentor.

Duncan's ineptitude with anything mechanical was legendary. Paul has described the difficulty of getting him to operate an automatic camera, and Frances Spalding relates how Duncan, when attempting to drive, "always looked startled by the noise of a car engine and seemed uncertain whether the car would move forwards, backwards or sideways." Even so, in 1955, he drove with Vanessa across France to Asolo where they rented the Marchesa Fossi's house "La Mura." Edward le Bas and Eardley Knollys soon joined them. Coming back through France, Duncan and Vanessa stopped at Alizay to visit their granddaughter Amaryllis, who was staying with a family there to learn French.

Back in London, they learned that their old friend Saxon Sydney-Turner was going into an old people's home so they took over his flat, moving back to Bloomsbury, at 28 Percy Street. That autumn Vanessa was a grandmother again, with the birth of Quentin and Olivier's first daughter, whom they named after Virginia Woolf. Despite a show at the Adams Gallery and the pied-à-terre in London, Vanessa's life was still centered at Charleston where she sought refuge in her painting.

Duncan, on the other hand, plunged back into larger projects. He was busy with the installation of his work at Lincoln Cathedral and back at work in the theatre again, designing scenery and costumes for a new production of John Blow's *Venus and Adonis*, first given at the Aldeburgh Festival on June 15 and later in September and October at the Scala Theatre in London. The production was by the English Opera Group, with Margaret Lensky and Heather Harper. Duncan received this commission through the suggestion of John Piper (b. 1903), an artist, writer and himself a noted designer for theatre. Piper designed many of Britten's operas, including *Death in Venice*, Covent Garden, 1973. Although Piper was an admirer of Duncan and Vanessa, Vanessa was not enthusiastic about his work.

On the day *Venus and Adonis* was to open, Vanessa and Duncan lunched with Benjamin Britten and the singer Peter Pears at their home, Red House. The relationship between Britten and Pears must have been interesting to Duncan, because of their life-long professional collaboration and loving and supportive relationship.

Never one to sit and feel sorry for himself, however, in Paul's absence Duncan was again active in meeting young men, and often found someone he liked on the train going to and from Charleston. Picasso's feat of picking up the teenage Marie-Thérèse, young enough to be his daughter, pales in comparison with Grant's ability to pick up boys young enough to be his grandchildren. In this period of his life, between the ages of sixty-nine and seventy-six, considering not only his age and physical vulnerability but the social and legal risks involved, he was remarkably unscathed by his adventures. It is difficult, if not impossible, for most people to imagine his audacity, never mind his facility in this specialized activity. Asked about this, Paul Roche said: "Duncan was like a vixen to young men." A combination of kindly paternalism and glittering coquetry, a sense of fun and sincere appreciation of the object of his attentions seem generally to have worked.

Duncan also continued to paint and travel with unflagging energy. Forty new paintings were exhibited at the Leicester Galleries in 1957, an exhibition shared with Anne Dunn. An old flame of Duncan's, Peter Morris, returned to England after twenty years abroad. Vanessa and Duncan were surprised to find he had aged from the rich, blue-green eyed, gilded youth they remembered from the 1920's into a gray-haired, older and poorer man. Still charming and affectionate, however, he joined Vanessa and Duncan in Venice that fall, with the old gang: Raymond Mortimer, Eardley Knollys, Clive and his companion Barbara Bagenal.

Vanessa, who often became close friends with Duncan's lovers, did not have the same tolerance for her men friends' women. Though she was by now indifferent to her husband, she treated Barbara with disdain. Clive took her rudeness in his stride. He continued his own separate and very active life, including visits to Picasso, and lunch with Somerset Maugham, as well as his life at Charleston as a country squire, tramping across the moors and shooting pheasants and other fowl which he would bring home to Charleston. Duncan liked to use them for still life subjects before handing them over to the kitchen.

The year 1958 was taken up with the installation of the murals in Lincoln Cathedral and preparations for "Duncan Grant: A Retrospective Exhibition," to be given at the Tate Gallery in May and June of 1959. Martin Butlin and Dennis Farr came to Charleston for lunch around the now-famous, decorated dining table, to discuss what work would be exhibited. They also visited Lydia Lopokova, now Lady Keynes, at nearby Tilton. Dennis Farr recalled with horror an unframed Picasso drawing on the mantelpiece, "fluttering...in the warm air currents thrown up by a blazing log fire." Lydia seemed oblivious to the danger.

Farr also remembers taking Vanessa and Clive around the exhibition at the Tate, and describes them as "somewhat tense." The detested John

Rothenstein was then director of the Tate, and no doubt they dreaded meeting him. Vanessa thought the selection of work "idiotic" and blamed Rothenstein's continuing animosity for it. E. M. Forster, a fan of Duncan's, also considered the show a disappointment, complaining that it included "none of Ben's [Britten's] sailors or of Harry Daley [Forster's policeman friend]." This exhibition was reviewed by Clive Bell, and was his last contribution to a newspaper. His support was as enthusiastic and appreciative as it had always been.

Vanessa contracted bronchial pleurisy early in 1959. Now in her eighties, she was already frail. In January 1960, she felt well enough to travel to Roquebrune with Duncan and their faithful housekeeper Grace Higgens. It was a gloomy visit, however, as they looked through the late Simon Bussy's paintings which his daughter Janie had put in order. Clive and Barbara arrived, staying in a nearby hotel in Menton, which did not improve Vanessa's mood, and it became clear she was no longer able to cope with practical matters. Duncan was alarmed by this and became untypically grumpy. Visits from Angelica, Peter Morris and Edward le Bas improved the mood, but after several months Vanessa complained that she could no longer bear Barbara Bagenal's presence and in early April she returned to Charleston.

Sad events piled up in London. Janie Bussy, a great favorite of both Clive and Vanessa, was found dead due to a gas leak in 51 Gordon Square. Dorothy Bussy, now senile, had to be placed in a nursing home where she died within a few weeks. Other old friends and lovers also died that year: Peter Morris' sister, Dora, and Douglas Davidson.

Although Vanessa visited the Picasso exhibition in the fall of 1960, that winter she never left the house. Clive went to Menton in the new year, leaving her and Duncan alone at Charleston. While in Menton, Clive fell and broke his leg. Kenneth Clark was staying nearby and saw to it that Clive was flown back to London where he entered the London Clinic. Vanessa was too weak to visit him there, but she expected him to return soon to Charleston.

Duncan and Vanessa read Jane Austen's *Mansfield Park* aloud to each other during March, and enjoyed the beautiful weather and early spring flowers. On April 4 Vanessa was again stricken with bronchitis which worsened daily. Quentin was with her on the morning of April 7, when she died quietly. Duncan had made two drawings of Vanessa on her deathbed, one before and one after she died. Angelica arived later in the day. Clive, still in the London Clinic, received the news from Barbara.

Duncan, who loved Vanessa and had relied on her love and attention for nearly fifty years, was devastated. It was not simply that someone of whom he was deeply fond was gone, but that the domestic pattern of his life was shattered. She was buried in Firle churchyard on April 12. It was a sad and lonely scene as Duncan, Quentin, Angelica and Grace saw her buried, without the comfort of any service. A plain black stone marks the grave, with only her name and dates on it. As Frances Spalding wrote "Its starkness is a reminder of her innate solitariness."[4]

---

[4]In *With Duncan Grant in Southern Turkey*, p. 21, Paul Roche writes that Duncan told him that shortly before Vanessa died, her son Quentin said to Duncan: "Tell her that you love her," and Duncan said: "I did. That was just before the end." Frances Spalding states this story is unfounded but Paul confirms that this is what Duncan told him. Duncan was eighty-eight years old when he told the story, and may have been meshing memories, projections and fantasies of that sad day.

CHAPTER 10

1961-1978

DUNCAN WAS IN A TERRIBLE STATE after Vanessa's death. To Paul Roche, he wired "Vanessa dead come back." Paul was in New York City, arranging for poetry readings, when he received the news. He responded without hesitation.

In America, based on the enthusiasm for his novel *O Pale Galilean,* Paul had been offered a teaching position at Smith College, where he joined a distinguished faculty including Sylvia Plath and Tony Hecht. While at Smith, Paul received a Bollingen Foundation Fellowship, with a stipend of $4000 to allow him to write. Wanting to make the money last as long as possible, Paul moved his family to Taxco, Mexico, where they lived very comfortably.

During this period abroad, Paul earned a living as a poet and began a successful career making new translations of Sophocles and Aeschylus, which were published by New American Library. He recorded for the Lamont Library at Harvard and the University of Chicago. His translation of *Antigone* was given on CBS in 1957. He had become a favorite of Gustav Davidson, head of the Poetry Society of America, who helped him give readings throughout the U.S.A. Even so, he earned very little and with a wife and four children to support he had no money for a ticket to England. To respond to Duncan's cry for help, he had to earn his passage by working on a ship sailing from Montreal.

In his eagerness to see Paul, Duncan met the ship at Tilbury and was overjoyed to see him. Duncan was still living in Percy Street, a house since pulled down, and the two men took up where they had left off. Paul has said, "It was a lovely, lovely time." He agreed to stay with Duncan for three months, to see him adjusted to his new situation.

Duncan then marshalled all his resources to promote Paul's career in England. A series of poetry readings were arranged, in very grand salons, through Duncan's aristocratic lady friends, particularly Lady Bridget Parsons and Lady Christabel Aberconway. These readings were great successes. At a poetry reading for the Duchess of Rutland, Paul's first publisher, Erica Marks of the Hand and Flower Press, offered a thousand pounds for the rights to publish the "Te Deum for Alfred J. Prufrock" (later presented on CBS in 1966). Paul wired at once to Clarissa who soon returned with the children.

Life back in chilly England, in a series of rented houses, each one more dismal than the last, with four small children to care for, was disillusioning and depressing to her. Things were greatly improved when they were able to buy a house, The Stables, The Street, Aldermaston, which cost about £3100, of which Duncan gave £1000, Paul's father gave £1000 and Erica Marks lent £1000. Over the next years, Paul and Clarissa created a lovely house and garden. It was to be Duncan's final address.

In London, Duncan moved to 24 Victoria Square, where he rented the top flat from Leonard Woolf. He also took a new lease on life, with Paul's love and loyalty helping him to overcome the loss of Vanessa.

Duncan continued his painting holidays abroad, now going to Spain, in 1962 and 1963. He stayed at Edward le Bas' house in Marbella, where Eardley Knollys and Edward "Teddy" Wolfe were fellow guests. (Teddy was the young South African painter found by Bunny Garnett in his bed at Charleston in 1919.) In April 1963, a retrospective exhibition of his work was held at the Minories, Colchester. In November 1964, Wildenstein & Co. showed "Duncan Grant and his World." In 1965 he spent May and June in Morocco.

Duncan visited the United States in 1966, where he stayed with George Bergen in New York. He also visited Yale University, where Paul gave a reading of his new translation of *Agamemnon* with the actress Pat Gilbert Read.

In April-May, 1966, "Painting by Duncan Grant and Vanessa Bell" was shown at the Royal West of England Academy in Bristol. Duncan returned to Morocco for the summer. That same year his friend Edward le Bas, nineteen years his junior, died. On his death, le Bas' sister (of Molyneux gown fame) immediately went to work to exorcise her brother's reputation of sexual stain. Edward and Duncan had delighted in exchanging erotic drawings and paintings, and there was great fear among mutual friends that the great store of Duncan's erotica, chez le Bas, might have been destroyed in the purge. It is believed, however, that one of Edward's faithful friends salvaged the collection before the Fury could reach it.

In 1967, Duncan showed twenty-seven works in an exhibition held from June to August in the Rye Art Gallery, Sussex, titled "Artists of Bloomsbury." That year he visited Greece with Paul, when Paul's translation of *Oedipus the*

King was made into a film starring Christopher Plummer, Lilli Palmer and Orson Welles. In the summer of 1968, he took a studio in Fez for two months. In 1969 he visited Holland, and that November there was "Portraits by Duncan Grant," an Arts Council exhibition, at Cambridge and Newcastle, Hull and Nottingham. In 1970, now eighty-five, Duncan moved to 3 Park Square West in London, visited Paris and Cyprus, and was made an Honorary Doctor of Letters by the Royal College of Art in London.

He was the subject of Christopher Mason's documentary film *Duncan Grant at Charleston,* made with financial support from the Marchioness of Dufferin and Ava. *The Times* wrote, "This is how personal portraits should be done on film, at once shrewd and affectionate, practical and poetic." In January and February of 1972 he was in Portugal and in May-April had a show at the Anthony d'Offay Gallery in London. He also collected another Honorary Doctorate, this time from the University of Sussex.

In this period of Duncan's life, from 1961 to 1973, Paul went back and forth to America, where he earned most of his income, particularly from poetry readings. When in England, he went to Charleston almost every week, often with his family, and spent much time with Duncan in London. One of Paul's first tasks on returning to England in 1961 and again later was to straighten out complications arising from Duncan's entanglements during his absence. Young men casually met and brought home to pose had on occasion stolen things from the studio, a clock from the mantelpiece and even Duncan's grandfather's kilts were taken. Fortunately, Duncan never seems to have encountered any violence and he was not really disturbed by the stealing.

The most serious case involved a young man who might have taken everything had he not been caught by the police after stealing silver from somebody else's house. After the arrest, along with the suitcase full of silver, about a dozen canvases by Duncan were found in his car. The police, correctly supposing they were also stolen property, visited Duncan, who, in his wish to protect the young man, said: "Oh, no, I gave them to him."

So the thief continued business as usual and eventually stole about 300 canvases. As Paul said, "There are a lot of good pictures floating around in the art world that came from him. He was a major source for certain London dealers." He sold a great number of these and had bought a house in Sussex on the proceeds. When the Sussex police were finally allowed to act, they retrieved perhaps 100 canvases and he was sent to jail. Paul then found himself put to work by Duncan, writing letters on the young man's behalf, trying to get him released from prison.

Grace Germany Higgens had been only sixteen years old when she came to work for Vanessa as maid and then nanny and ultimately cook-housekeeper. She was called "the angel of Charleston" and was credited by everybody for her ability to keep the house, against all odds and in strangest of circumstances, in beautiful running order. While she was there the rooms were clean, the beds with their fresh linen were turned down at night, with hot water bottles tucked in. Guests would be asked what they wanted for breakfast the night before and whatever was asked for was provided. When she left after nearly 50 years of service, there was great concern about who would look after Charleston and Duncan and Clive, its two elderly tenants.

A young couple was engaged, but the man did not do his part, which essentially was to be the gardener. He seemed to take over the place as his own, converting a studio and an out-building into garages for his motorbikes. Though both Duncan and Paul liked the young couple personally, the arrangement did not work. Duncan, as usual, wanted no unpleasantness, so Paul eventually fired the couple. But Angelica hired them back, saying Paul mustn't be unfair. They stayed a few years longer, as the garden and its paths became choked with weeds.

The gardens at Charleston[1] were designed by Duncan, who was a keen gardener. He was always buying plants and trees, and he planted a deep red rose with a lovely heavy scent (Papa Melland) along the east wall of the garden. He found a pretty reed which he thought would go well in the pond (which has been the subject of so many paintings—Number 56). The plant loved the pond all too well and by the 1960's it had choked it so thoroughly that no water could be seen. Paul floated out into the middle of the pond in an old tin tub but could make no headway in clearing out the mat of tangled roots. He and his son Tobit (Number 23) gardened at Charleston, rediscovering a walnut tree Duncan had planted years before, which they resurrected from engulfing brambles.

Clarissa came to love Duncan, and the Roches felt at home with him at Charleston, adding perhaps to Angelica's feeling of deprivation. Many years later, when Clarissa had an idea to decorate tables in the Omega manner, after Duncan's designs, Angelica threatened to sue her.

Duncan maintained his friendships in London, and continued to make new friends. His tiff with Christabel Aberconway, wife of the chairman of the

---

[1]The gardens have been restored through a grant from Lila Acheson Wallace, co-founder of the *Reader's Digest*.

firm that built the liner the *Queen Mary,* was long past, and she also became a friend of Paul's. She was still a leading hostess, giving an annual party for the most select of London's smart set at her house in North Audley Street. The house was like an art gallery, its walls hung with paintings by Cézanne, Matisse, and Picasso. Paul gave a reading of his translation of Sappho at her house. Sometimes he and Christabel would go to the cinema alone, sometimes with Duncan.

Kenneth Clark continued to be a patron and good friend, and was encouraging about Paul's poetry. Duncan and Paul visited him for tea at his flat in Albany, and also lunched with him at his castle at Hythe.

A great new friend was a very pretty young woman called Lindy, Belinda Guinness. She was to marry Sheridan Frederick Terence Hamilton-Temple-Blackwood, The Marquess of Dufferin and Ava. She came from a remarkable family and was a niece of Diana Cooper and granddaughter of the Duchess of Rutland. She soon developed a passion for Duncan and his work and he responded in a most remarkable way: he loved her. Duncan was often at her house in Hans Crescent in London, and visited her at Candelboye, County Down, in Ireland. She owned many of his pictures (Number 46), and was extremely kind to him in his old age. At Charleston, the toilet near his studio was "a horrible little hole," which she had completely done up, including a little bar he could hold onto for balance.

His relationships with grand ladies were not always carefree. Lady Cadogan asked Duncan, when he was well into his eighties, to alter a portrait he had done of her husband Alexander, perhaps an adjustment of the lower lip. Paul knew something was wrong when Duncan began to say, "I can't be at lunch with you today because I've got to go to Lady Cadogan's." Finally he admitted she wanted the portrait changed. The head began to shrink as he worked on it until it came to resemble the Loch Ness monster. Duncan finally gave up and let Angelica have a go at it. But she too failed. Duncan, with Paul for moral support, finally returned the portrait to its owner. Paul said exposing the canvas to her was difficult. He finally had to rip the cover off, like taking off a bandage. Lady Cadogan could not restrain her first impression which was: "OH! It's horrible!" Paul and Duncan fled before she could say any more.

In 1973, when Duncan was eighty-eight, it was decided between them that Paul would give up his work abroad and devote himself completely to taking care of Duncan. As Paul had to give up his source of income, Duncan gave him a small salary. Paul had by now published thirteen volumes of prose, poetry and translations, and his translations of Greek and Latin drama had become popular as college texts. He had won the di Castognola Award of the

Poetry Society of America and the Bartlett Award of the Poetry Society in London. However, he realized clearly that what was most important to him was to be with Duncan while there was still time. There were to be five more years of travel, pleasure and important creative work for Duncan. This was undoubtedly possible because of the strong and consistent support he received from Paul.

That year, after studying glossy travel brochures, the two set off by air for Turkey. Sixty-five years before, Duncan had visited Istanbul with Maynard Keynes. On this trip, he and Paul visited Antalya, Side, Kemer and Graeco-Roman sites. Duncan painted every day while Paul sunbathed. Paul's book *With Duncan Grant in Southern Turkey* gives a charming picture of the fun they had together.

Also in January 1973, the Fermoy Art Gallery in King's Lynn showed "Recent Paintings: Duncan Grant." Lady Fermoy, Lady-in-Waiting to the Queen Mother and grandmother of Diana, Princess of Wales, was the wife of Edmund Maurice Roche, The Baron Fermoy. Lady Fermoy had a house in King's Lynn, where Duncan and Paul were her guests before the opening. For this show Queen Elizabeth the Queen Mother lent her two "St. Paul's Cathedral" pictures of 1939 and 1947. But most of the other pictures dealt with favorite themes, now including Morocco as well as Charleston, and most had been painted in the 1970's. They are astonishing in their beauty and power, as if Duncan had distilled the revelations of a lifetime of exploration and versatility. Several of these show work of artists whom Duncan admired. "Still Life with Nijinsky" features the Druet photograph, "Still Life with Matisse" shows an illustration of one of Matisse's large, cut-out gouaches, and "Still Life with Sharaku" contains a work by the 18th-century Japanese artist Toshusai Sharaku.

Duncan's work always sold well but, considering his past celebrity, his prices were now remarkably low. Any painter with an international reputation, and whose vanity was attached to the monetary value of his work, could never have survived the humiliation of Duncan's debased position in the art market. Duncan was always pleased when anyone wanted his work. One happy aspect of this was that people of limited means, who loved his work for itself, were able to acquire his pictures. The Fermoy show prices ranged from £300 to £750. "Still Life with Matisse" (Number 105), which the Queen Mother bought, was priced at only £400.

In 1974, Paul and Duncan set off for Scotland, to visit The Doune, the Grant family house at Rothiemurchus, where Duncan was born. At the end of a long avenue, they found the great house in a state of near ruin, having been used as a barn. Duncan would not enter the house but made sketches, and walked around, pointing out that the field of weeds stretching down to the River Spey had been immaculate lawns, where he had played cricket as a boy. Despite a certain sadness, Duncan lived entirely in the present and accepted it. He welcomed the fact that he had this rich past, but he never mourned for it.

Tuesday, January 21, 1975, was Duncan's ninetieth birthday. He had lived long enough to become a celebrity again. He received many birthday greetings, including a celebratory poem from Noël Annan, then Provost of the Slade, saying, "no man subtler than you still paints." A half-page picture of him had appeared on the front page of the Arts section of *The Sunday Times*, with remarks by Raymond Mortimer, and his picture was also in *The Times* on Tuesday. Mortimer wrote, "In 1914, . . . his friendliness, charm, good looks and original talk endeared him even to those who found his work incomprehensibly modern. . . . He remains delightful, and modest also. Good critics singled out the youthful Grant as the most gifted of the artists here who had been influenced by the Paris Post-Impressionists. Later, when our other painters were growing less realistic, he became more so, swimming against the current to the vexation of most critics. Today he wins increasing applause from young painters who work in a contrasting tradition. Having admired him and his work for over fifty years, I know that, though a keen enjoyer, he has never been distracted by alcohol, smart society, indolence, the demands of dealers or the other temptations that have enfeebled so many of the most promising painters. Regardless of fashion, he has always obeyed his own eyes and his own imagination."

The d'Offay Gallery showed "Recent Paintings," and later had another show of early work. "Paintings and Drawings by Duncan Grant" were shown at the Southover Gallery in Lewes, Suffolk. In February-March was the Ninetieth Birthday Exhibition at the Tate Gallery, with other exhibitions at the Scottish National Gallery of Modern Art, the Museum of Modern Art in Oxford, Towner Gallery of Art in Eastbourne, Gallery Edward Harvane, and Davis & Long in New York City.

Despite having to use a wheelchair, Duncan went to Tangier in October, where he and Paul had been lent the palatial house of Rex Nan Kivell, a wealthy man who had made money as a dealer, through the Redfern Gallery, one of London's most successful galleries. Although Rex had never exhibited Duncan's work, he greatly admired it.

The villa, El Farah, with its splendid gardens, overlooked the sea. The place was supposed to be looked after by a caretaker and his wife, who never appeared—the first sign of problems to come. Despite the sunny days, the nights are very cold in Tangier, but the one available servant told Paul he couldn't turn on the heat without permission from the agent. The agent claimed there was no oil for the central heating. It was clear to Paul that Rex was being cheated in all matters to do with the house. He sent a wire to Rex: "For God's sake can we have the central heating turned on?" The heating was then turned on spasmodically but by then Duncan had caught pneumonia. He took to his bed and was soon at the point of dying.

Paul called a doctor who lived in Tangier, Dr. Anderson, a Scotsman, who began prescribing for Duncan. One afternoon as Paul was pacing on the terrace, the doctor came to him to discuss funeral arrangements. Paul was aghast. He was determined that Duncan was not going to die.

How to make him warm enough was his first concern, as the heating was still not turned on. They were using two rooms of the house, a dining room which they had turned into a studio and an oblong room next to it as a bedroom. There was an enormous fireplace and Paul dragged back to the house with him the six foot long branches of a eucalyptus tree. He started a roaring fire and kept it going night and day with more huge eucalyptus logs. The servant wouldn't help him, afraid, no doubt, of the damage being done to the room as the smoke from the fire blackened the ceiling and the precious tiles on the wall.

Duncan came through the pneumonia, to Anderson's surprise, but was still deathly ill and became suicidal. He asked the doctor what was the easiest way to kill himself. Paul had nursed Duncan throughout the ordeal and could not understand why, now that he had survived the pneumonia, Duncan was not completely himself. So, he took stool samples to the Spanish Hospital for analysis, where a hemorrhage was suggested but not found. Paul decided Duncan was dying of poisoning from constipation. This proved to be correct and was easily remedied. Duncan bounced back, with his love of life restored, and he was a new man.

Even ill, Duncan never rested from his life long habit of work. In his delirium he asked for a pair of scissors and Paul found him cutting up Rex's blankets and sheets. He asked him what he was doing. Duncan replied, "I'm getting ready for a show in Japan, they've asked me to submit a series of designs." Another time, while still ill, Paul discovered Duncan on the floor in front of one of Rex's superb chairs, upholstered in faun-colored velvet, drawing designs on the velvet with a ball point pen in the best Omega fashion.

When Duncan was better, Paul brought him into the dining room and sat him at the magnificent roseburl table, where he drew and painted. One day he spilled a little paint on the table and damaged the surface trying to scrape it off with a knife. Also, the table had warped from the intense heat of Paul's fire.

"Perhaps we could cover it with a sheet," Duncan suggested, and they waited like naughty children for their punishment.

As Duncan recovered they began to enjoy themselves. Paul would get a fresh fish in the market every day and gather wild asparagus. Occasionally they invited Alec Waugh for dinner. They were reading his *Loom of Youth*, written when he was seventeen, which they both found wonderful. In time, Rex arrived with his entourage and generously forgave everything, perhaps blaming himself for the trouble caused by his agent.

In May 1976, they returned to England. An exhibition of work done mostly in Tangier was shown at the Southover Gallery in Lewes and the next year an exhibition was held at the Rye Art Gallery.

In October 1977, Paul decided it would be more comfortable for Duncan to live with him and his family at The Stables in Aldermaston, where the house was well heated and it would be easier to care for him. Paul had built a special sun room for Duncan, and filled it with geraniums and sweet-smelling, flowering plants. Some of Duncan's favorite things were there with him, including Druet's 1910 photograph of Nijinsky (Number 66). A tame canary flew about and sometimes perched on the artist. The room was sunny and Duncan would wear a great straw hat with a long turkey feather stuck in it as he worked in his wheelchair, which had a special drawing board Paul had fixed to fit across its arms.

Recalling much earlier work done at the height of the Omega period, for example his 1915 "In Memoriam Rupert Brooke" (Number 52), Duncan started working with abstractions in rectangular shapes (Number 53). Perhaps these pictures reflected presentiments of his approaching death.

Thanks to Richard Morphet, a plan was made to send Duncan to Paris to see the great exhibition "The Last Ten Years of Cézanne," at the Grand Palais. Some fifty-three years before, Duncan and Vanessa had gone to see the Pellerin collection of Cézannes in Paris. Roger Fry was writing an article on them, which later became his book *Cézanne*. In 1913, when they had gone to Paris, they left Marjorie Strachey in charge of Vanessa's "summer school," put together for Angelica and a few other little children of friends, including Anastasia and Igor Anrep, Judith Bagenal, and Christopher and Nicholas Henderson.

Now, in 1976, Sir Nicholas Henderson was the British Ambassador in France. So it was arranged that Duncan be invited to Paris for three days as his guest. Duncan and Paul were met at the airport by the Embassy's Rolls-Royce and installed in splendid rooms at the Embassy, which was once the palace of the Empress Joséphine and still filled with her furniture. Duncan was delighted to find the sideboard in his room stocked with the very best claret, gin, vodka and whiskeys.

At the Grand Palais, Duncan spent a good two hours at the exhibition. In his wheelchair, with Paul, Quentin Bell, Pandora and Cordelia Roche taking turns pushing, he gazed and gazed at the pictures, obviously moved and inspired.

On his last night in Paris, Duncan tossed himself out of bed because of a dream. "Oh, I have to catch a train to Cambridge to meet Maynard," he told Paul, who found him shivering on the floor in the morning. He was shaken by the fall and a chill followed.

Back in Aldermaston, Duncan was still in good spirits and said he felt inspired by his visit. He began and finished a little painting, but pneumonia was taking hold. One other advantage of moving Duncan to The Stables, The Street, Aldermaston, was that an excellent doctor lived directly across the road, Dr. Robert Cooper. He saw Duncan and then gently told Paul that the end was near. Paul called Angelica and Quentin to tell them. Angelica was then at Charleston and Quentin lived nearby. They came at once to Aldermaston. Duncan was now speechless because of his bronchitis but Angelica described him as being perfectly self-possessed and alive to all that was going on. She wrote, "He never appeared to suffer, either from his physical ailments or from his necessary dependence on others."[2] Of course, he was fortunate that his dependence lay with people who loved him and were attentive to his every comfort.

Paul at first refused to accept Dr. Cooper's opinion, thinking that Duncan could be revived as he had been in Tangier. However, Duncan was weaker now and there was a difference. His body seemed to be breaking up. The doctor saw that it should not be prolonged. At first, Paul couldn't accept that. He wanted an oxygen mask brought to keep Duncan alive. Dr. Cooper was right that Duncan could never have painted again, never have been fully himself again. Paul thinks that Duncan had decided, after the pilgrimage to Cézanne, that there couldn't be a better time to go. Paul said, "So he lived, right up to the hilt, to the very end, you see." Angelica wrote: ". . . Paul rang to say Duncan had died quietly and peacefully; just the way one expected him to go—Duncan never did anything painfully."[3]

Duncan Grant died, at the age of ninety-three, at The Stables, Aldermaston, on Tuesday, May 9th, 1978.[4] Paul, in deep distress, was appalled by the coffin which was brought to The Stables for Duncan's body, and was sure

---

[2]*Deceived with Kindness*, by Angelica Bell, p. 9.

[3]Op. cit. p. 10.

[4]The date of death as reported in the *New York Times* obituary by John Russell was incorrect, and the London *Times* was wrong too.

Duncan would have hated to be put in it. So in the best Omega tradition, the brass was stripped off, the box itself painted white and Pandora Roche painted garlands of flowers on it. Lady Freyberg sent red roses to The Stables and these were placed on the coffin for its trip to the cemetery.

Duncan was buried in the little churchyard at Firle, next to Vanessa Bell.[5] There was a small group of mourners, which included Paul and Clarissa with Tobit, Pandora, Martin, Vanessa and Cordelia, Angelica, Quentin and his wife, Grace and Walter Higgens, and Angus Davidson.[6]

A splendid memorial service was held in Saint Paul's Cathedral, at noon on Tuesday, June 27, 1978. There was music by Mozart, Purcell, and Bach. Paul Roche read his poem "The Artist." The eulogy was delivered by Lord Clark of Saltwood.[7] The bidding was beautifully appropriate:

"We come together to give thanks to God for Duncan Grant—from first to last and all the time an artist, generous and whole-hearted in his response to all that could engage his genius, richly endowed to express his many-splendoured vision. As we call to mind his art, we remember also his gift for making and keeping friends, suffusing his own life and theirs with a spontaneous, unselfconscious delight in all things of man's making or imagining...."

---

[5]Paul thinks they had decided long before to be buried next to each other.

[6]Duncan's favorite, sixty years before.

[7]Familiar to a vast audience through his television series "Civilisation."

DUNCAN GRANT

by Lord Clark

IT IS VERY DIFFICULT to think of Duncan Grant in relation to death. No man I have ever met was more happily alive. In the forty-five years I knew him I never saw him looking sad or depressed. When painting he would be quiet and concentrated, but the moment he laid down his brush, he would be prepared for a giggle. Although we saw him almost every week, we sometimes moved into a different world, and my stories about the *beau monde* delighted him. He was entirely without envy, either socially or artistically.

I cannot remember him speaking critically about another artist; like Turner, he knew how difficult it was. He often spoke tolerantly about a painter whom I had considered worthless. In this he was very different from Vanessa Bell, and from Bloomsbury in general, where the critical sense was somewhat overdeveloped. Indeed it seemed like a happy accident that Duncan had been adopted as, so to say, the official painter of Bloomsbury. There were some long faces in Gordon Square, and without Duncan Grant, the style of painting might have been equally angular. Fortunately Clive Bell, the leading critic of the group, was also very jolly.

Why did Bloomsbury take Duncan up? I think it must have been largely through the influence of Roger Fry, who recognized that he was the only painter in England since Sickert whose work could be shown without embarrassment to a cultivated Frenchman. When Fry first praised them, he was painting quasi-abstract decorative pictures of the kind that fitted in well with Fry's theories. But no one who loved life and visual experience as much as Duncan did could have remained an abstract painter for long, and very soon flowers began to appear on his canvases, and seductive nudes in pastel on large sheets of paper. Roger Fry accepted them, although he may secretly have wished that Duncan had stuck to his brown and green still lives, which to some extent he did, painting seriously worked out pictures which were hard to distinguish from those of Vanessa. One might think they were painted to placate Roger, but in fact Roger was a great believer in Duncan's gifts as a decorator, and in particular as a scene designer, and when Glyndebourne's first productions revealed some very commonplace stage sets, I did my best to persuade John Christie to employ his neighbor—without success. What a different Duncan we might have known if he had become, so to say, resident scene designer at Glyndebourne. But I doubt if it would ever have worked, largely because by that time Duncan had become less experimental and wanted to concentrate on his own way of painting. This truth dawned on me when Duncan executed his largest commission, the decorations of the *Queen Mary*. I had imagined that they would be in a light, fluid style. Instead they were carried through with a masterly fullness. They were rejected by the chairman's wife, Lady Bates, and have seldom been seen.

After the war Duncan and Vanessa spent most of their time in the country, near Lewes, and in consequence Duncan became more and more a landscape painter and very good landscapes they were, but there have often been good English landscape painters, but none with Duncan Grant's finesse and invention. There is no happier life, and for this reason, or because they have to be in the open air, landscape painters tend to live to a good age. All the obituaries spoke of Duncan as the last of the Bloomsburies; in a literal sense this is true enough, but if the word has any meaning (and I fancy it has a little) Duncan was completely outside the Bloomsbury ethos. He was sweet, gay, uncritical, and charming. There, at last, I have used the word which most people use first in talking about him. There was an overwhelming charm in his glance, his giggle, his frequent movements (he was the least monumental of men). Alas, that quality has gone from us, but we can still see it in his sketches. There we may find the grace, the gaiety, the love of beauty in its simplest form, that was his birthright and shone out in all his being. And there is some evidence of real greatness, which shows that Roger Fry and Clive Bell were right when they picked out Duncan Grant as the hope of English painting.

Appendix

WORKS BY DUNCAN GRANT IN NORTH AMERICAN PUBLIC
COLLECTIONS Compiled by Patricia L. Boutelle, Curator, Long Beach
Museum of Art

Art Gallery of Ontario, Toronto
 "Gladioli," n.d.
 "Farm Pond near Firle, Sussex," n.d.
Art Institute of Chicago
 "Seated Nude by Fireplace," n.d.
Boston Museum of Fine Arts
 "Waterloo Bridge," n.d.
Metropolitan Museum of Art, New York City
 "Coffee Pot," 1916 (see book jacket back cover)
 "Vanessa Bell," 1931
 "Artist's Study at Charleston," 1967 (see Number 75)
Santa Barbara Museum of Fine Arts
 "Portrait of David Garnett," 1916
Smith College Museum of Art
 "Cardplayer," n.d.
Toledo Museum of Art
 "A Sussex Farm," 1936 (see Number 71)
Vancouver Art Gallery, British Columbia
 "Sun Flowers and Dahlias," 1930
Yale Center for British Art, New Haven
 "Pamela," 1911 (see Plate 39)
 "Two Nudes on a Beach," n.d. (see Number 60)
 "At Eleanor: Vanessa Bell," 1915
 "In Memoriam: Rupert Brooke," 1915 (see Number 52)
 "Study of Hands," n.d.
 "Study of Feet," n.d.

Bibliography

Annan, Noel, *Leslie Stephen*, MacGibbon & Kee, 1951.

Anscombe, Isabelle, *Omega and After, Bloomsbury and the Decorative Arts*, Thames & Hudson, 1981.

Askwith, Betty, *Two Victorian Families*, Chatto & Windus, 1971.

Austen, Jane, *Mansfield Park*.

Baron, Wendy, *Ethel Sands and Her Circle*.

Beaumont, C. W., *The Diaghilev Ballet in London*, Putnam, 1940.

Bell, Clive *Art*, Chatto and Windus, 1914.

    Since Cézanne, Chatto & Windus, 1922.

    Civilization, Chatto and Windus, 1928.

    Old Friends. Personal Recollections, Chatto and Windus, 1956.

Bell, Quentin *Bloomsbury*, Futura Publications, 1974.

Vanessa Bell's Family Album, compiled by Quentin Bell and Angelica Garnett, Jill Norman & Hobhouse, 1981.

Bloomfield, Paul, *Uncommon People: A Study of England's Elite*, Hamish Hamilton, 1955.

The Bloomsbury Group—The Word and the Image, The National Book League/The Hogarth Press, 1976.

El Grup de Bloomsbury, catalogue for Fundacio Caixa de Pensions, 1986.

Boswell, John, *Christianity, Social Tolerance, and Homosexuality. Gay People in Western Europe from the Beginning of the Christian Era to the Fourteenth Century*, University of Chicago Press, 1980.

Boyd, Elizabeth French, *Bloomsbury Heritage*, Hamish Hamilton, 1976.

Buckle, Richard, *Diaghilev*, Atheneum, 1979.

    Nijinsky, Weidenfeld & Nicolson, 1971.

Burne-Jones, Georgiana, *Memorials of Edward Burne-Jones*, 2 vols, Macmillan, 1904.

Carpenter, E., *The Art of Creation, Essays on the Self and Its Powers*, Macmillan, 1917.

Carrington, Dora, *Letters and Extracts from Her Diaries*, ed. David Garnett, Oxford University Press, 1979.

Charleston, Letters, Manuscripts and Documents to be sold for the benefit of The Charleston Trust, catalogue, Sotheby's 21 July 1980.

The Charleston Artists: Vanessa Bell, Duncan Grant and Their Friends, catalogue, Meadows Museum, Dallas, 1984.

Clark, Kenneth, *Another Part of the Wood*, John Murray, 1974.
  Civilisation, A Personal View, Harper & Row, 1969.
  The Nude.
  The Other Half, John Murray, 1977.
Collins, Judith, *The Omega Workshops*, Secker & Warburg, 1984.
Constable, W. G., "Duncan Grant," *British Artists of Today*, no. VI, 1927.
Cooper, Lady Diana, *The Rainbow Comes and Goes*, Hart-Davis, 1958.
Cooper, Emmanuel, *The Sexual Perspective*.
Coote, Stephen, ed., *The Penguin Book of Homosexual Verse*, Penguin, 1986.
Deacon, Richard, *The Cambridge Apostles*, Robert Royce, 1985.
Elderfield, John, *Matisse: In the Collection of the Museum of Modern Art*, Museum of
  Modern Art, 1978.
Ede, H. S., *Savage Messiah*, Heinemann, 1931.
Edel, Leon, *Bloomsbury: A House of Lions*, The Hogarth Press, 1979.
Forster, E. M., *G. Lowes Dickinson*, Edward Arnold, 1934.
Fry, Roger, *Duncan Grant*, Leonard and Virginia Woolf, 1930.
  Cézanne, Hogarth Press, 1927.
Gadd, David, *The Loving Friends. A Portrait of Bloomsbury*, Hogarth Press, 1974.
Garnett, Angelica, *Deceived with Kindness, A Bloomsbury Childhood*, Chatto &
  Windus/The Hogarth Press, 1984.
  "Duncan Grant," in *Duncan Grant* (1885-1978), exhibition catalogue, Anthony
    d'Offay Gallery, Nov-Dec. 1981.
Garnett, David, *The Golden Echo*, Chatto & Windus, 1953.
  The Flowers of the Forest, Chatto & Windus, 1955.
  The Familiar Faces, Chatto & Windus, 1962.
Garnett, David, ed., *The White/Garnett Letters*, Jonathan Cape, 1968.
Gathorne-Hardy, Jonathan, *The Old School Tie, The Phenomenon of the English Public
  School*, Viking, 1978.
Gibson, Ian, *The English Vice, Beating, Sex and Shame in Victorian England and After*,
  Duckworth, 1978.
The Engraved Work of Eric Gill, Her Majesty's Stationery Office, 1963.
Grant, Elizabeth, *Memoirs of a Highland Lady*, ed. by Lady Strachey, rev. edn. by
  Angus Davidson, John Murray, 1950.
Grant, Bartle, ed., *The Receipt Book of Elizabeth Raper, with Portions of Her Cipher
  Journal*. Portrait and Decorations by Duncan Grant, Nonesuch Press, 1924.
Grant, Duncan, "Virginia Woolf," in *Horizon*, June 1941.
"Duncan Grant. Three Paintings," in *The Dial*, November 1922.
Paintings by Duncan Grant from 1910 to 1929, catalogue, Paul Guillaume Gallery,
  1929.
Duncan Grant. Recent Paintings, catalogue, with a foreword by David Garnett,
  Cooling Galleries, 1931.
Duncan Grant. Drawings, catalogue, with a foreword by Kenneth Clark, Thos.
  Agnew & Sons, 1933.
Duncan Grant. A Retrospective Exhibition, catalogue, with an introductory essay by
  Alan Clutton-Brock, The Tate Gallery, 1959.

Duncan Grant and His World, catalogue, with an introduction by Denys Sutton, Wildenstein & Co., 1964.

Portraits by Duncan Grant, catalogue, with an introduction by Richard Shone, Arts Council (Great Britain), 1969.

Duncan Grant. Watercolours and Drawings, catalogue, with a note by Stephen Spender. d'Offay Couper Gallery, 1972.

Duncan Grant. Recent Paintings, catalogue, Fermoy Art Gallery, 1973.

Duncan Grant. A Display to Celebrate His Ninetieth Birthday, catalogue, with notes by Richard Morphet, Tate Gallery, 1975.

Duncan Grant. A Ninetieth Birthday Exhibition of Paintings, catalogue, with an introduction by David Brown, Scottish National Gallery of Modern Art.

Duncan Grant and Bloomsbury, catalogue, with an introduction by Richard Shone, The Fine Art Society (Edinburgh), 1975.

Duncan Grant, catalogue, Davis & Long Co., 1975.

Duncan Grant, catalogue, with a tribute by Paul Roche, Rye Art Gallery, 1977.

Duncan Grant—Designer, ed. Richard Shone and Judith Collins, Bluecoat Gallery, Liverpool, 1980.

Duncan Grant. Works on Paper, catalogue, d'Offay Gallery, 1981.

Grant, Patrick, *The Good Old Days*, Thames & Hudson, 1956.

Graves, Robert, *Goodbye to All That*, Jonathan Cape 1929.

Grigoriev, S. L., *The Diaghilev Ballet 1909-1929*, trs. by Vera Bowen, Constable, 1953.

Hamnett, Nina, *Laughing Torso: Reminiscences*, Constable, 1932.

Heilbrun, Carolyn, *Toward a Recognition of Androgyny*, Knopf, 1973.

Hession, Charles H., *John Maynard Keynes*, Macmillan, 1984.

History of Modern Painting, ed. Germain Bazin, Heinemann, 1951.

Hockney, David, *David Hockney*, Abrams, 1977.

Holroyd, Michael, *Augustus John*, 2 vols., 1974.

 Lytton Strachey: A Critical Biography, 2 vols., Holt, Rinehart, Winston 1967-68.

Hyde, H. M., *The Love That Dared Not Speak Its Name*, Little, Brown, 1970.

John, Augustus, *Chiaroscuro: Fragments of an Autobiography*, Jonathan Cape, 1952.

Johnstone, J. K., *The Bloomsbury Group*, Secker & Warburg, 1954.

Keynes, John Maynard, *Two Memoirs*, with an introduction by David Garnett, Hart-Davis, 1949.

Koestler, A., *The Act of Creation*, Macmillan, 1964.

Laura Ashley Home Furnishings 1987, catalogue.

Lehmann, John, *Thrown to the Woolfs*, Weidenfeld & Nicolson, 1978.

Lewis, Wyndham, *Blasting and Bombardiering*, Calder & Boyars, 1967.

Lydia Lopokova, ed. Milo Keynes, St. Martin's, 1983.

Moore, G. E., *Principia Ethica*, Cambridge University Press, 1903.

The Early Memoirs of Lady Ottoline Morrell, Robert Gathorne-Hardy, ed., Faber & Faber, 1963.

Morphet, Richard, "The Significance of Charleston," *Apollo*, November 1967, pp. 342-45.

Mortimer, Raymond, *Duncan Grant*, Penguin Books, 1948.

The Omega Workshops 1913-19: Decorative Arts of Bloomsbury, catalogue, Crafts Council, 1983.

Penrose, Barrie, and Simon Freeman, *Conspiracy of Silence, The Secret Life of Anthony Blunt*, Grafton Books, 1986.

Pickvance, Ronald, "Duncan Grant and His World," *Apollo*, November 1964, p. 409.

Raverat, G., *Period Piece*, Norton, 1976.

Reade, Brian, ed., *Sexual Heretics, Male Homosexuality in English Literature from 1850-1900*, Coward-McCann, 1971.

Roche, Paul, *With Duncan Grant in Southern Turkey*, Honeyglen, 1982.

"Duncan Grant," in *The Transatlantic Review*, Number 51, Spring 1975.

Rothenstein, John, *Modern English Painters*, 3 vols, Eyre and Spottiswoode, 1952-74.

Rowse, A. L., *Homosexuals in History, A Study of Ambivalence in Society, Literature and the Arts*, Weidenfeld & Nicolson, 1977.

Shell Guide to Scotland.

Shone, Richard, *The Murals, Berwick Church*, Towner Art Gallery, 1969.

Bloomsbury Portraits. Vanessa Bell, Duncan Grant and Their Circle, Phaidon, 1976.

The Century of Change, British Painting Since 1900, Phaidon, 1977.

Sinclair, Andrew, *The Red and the Blue*.

Spalding, Frances, *Vanessa Bell*, Ticknor & Fields, 1983.

Spender, Stephen, *World Within World*, Hamish Hamilton 1951.

Stephen, Adrian, *The "Dreadnought" Hoax*, Leonard and Virginia Woolf, 1936.

Strachey, Lytton, *Ermyntrude and Esmeralda*, with illustrations by Erte, Stein & Day, 1969.

Sutton, Denis, "Jacques Copeau and Duncan Grant," *Apollo*, August 1967, pp. 138-41.

Vanggaard, Thorkill, *Phallos, a Symbol and Its History in the Male World*, International Universities Press, 1972.

von Wright, G. H., *Ludwig Wittgenstein: Letters of Russell, Keynes and Moore*, Basil Blackwell, 1974.

Watney, Stephen, *English Post-Impressionism*, Studio Vista, 1980.

Waugh, Alec, *Loom of Youth*.

Weeks, Jeffrey, *Coming Out: Homosexual Politics in Britain from the 19th Century to the Present*, Quartet Books, London, 1977.

Woolf, Leonard, *Growing*, Hogarth Press, 1961.

Sowing, Hogarth Press, 1961.

Beginning Again, Hogarth Press, 1964.

Downhill all the Way, Hogarth Press, 1967.

The Journey not the Arrival That Matters, Hogarth Press, 1969.

Woolf, Virginia, *Moments of Being*, ed. Jeanne Schulkind, Sussex University Press, 1976.

A Room of One's Own, Triad/Panther Books, 1977.

Index

PLATES 1-64

(All photographs 1-28 are from the collection of Paul Roche, except as noted.)

PLATE 1

1. Duncan Grant, c. 1897, at Hillbrow Preparatory School, Rugby.

2. Duncan Grant, c. 1902.

PLATE 2

3. Duncan Grant, possibly at Streatley-on-Thames, c. 1902-3.

5. Duncan Grant, posing.

4. Duncan Grant, playing pipes, c. 1902-3.

6. Duncan Grant, as a Spanish dancer, in the walled garden at Charleston. (The Tate Archive, London)

7. Duncan Grant, 1946, wearing turban at Taviton Street, photo by Paul Roche.

PLATE 3

8. Quentin Bell in foreground, l. to r. Edward "Teddy" Wolfe, Osbert Sitwell, Duncan Grant, May 1919. (The Tate Archive, London)

9. Duncan Grant and Maynard Keynes.

(The Tate Archive, London)

10. Clive Bell in background reading, with his sons Julian and Quentin sitting on Maynard Keynes' lap, West Wittering, 1915.

11. Vanessa Bell with Angelica, on the beach at St. Tropez, c. 1921.

(The Tate Archive, London)

12. l. to r. Judith Stephen, Duncan Grant holding kitten, with his daughter Angelica, Charleston, c. 1923.

13. l. to r. Duncan Grant, Angelica, Roger Fry, at Charleston, c. 1925.

PLATE 4

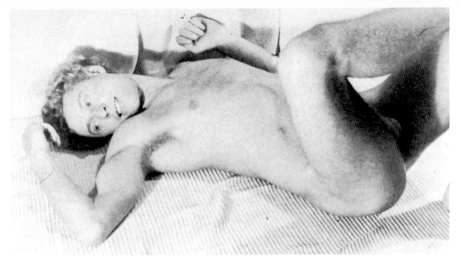

14. Paul Roche, 1946.

15. Paul Roche in sailor suit, at Taviton Street, 1946, photo by Duncan Grant.

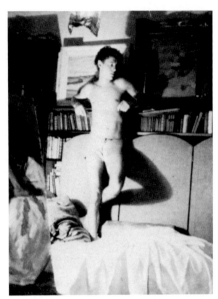

16. Paul Roche, posing at Taviton Street, 1946. Note Duncan Grant's canvas in left foreground and, behind Paul's left elbow, Vanessa Bell's "Iceland Poppies," 1908, one of the earliest of her works still in existenc

17. Toni Asserati, a model, at Charleston.

18. A model, at Charleston.

PLATE 5

19. Duncan's mother, Ethel Grant, seated in the center of the group, with her sisters and friends.

20. Duncan Grant with Violet Hammersley, photo by Elizabeth Winn. (collection of Elizabeth Winn)

21. Paul and Clarissa Roche, with their children Martin, Pandora, Vanessa and Cordelia, at Aldermaston, 1968.

22. Duncan Grant with Martin and Vanessa Roche, on the beach at Hythe.

23. Tobit Roche in foreground, with Paul Roche, Duncan Grant in wheelchair, and Richard Morphet's daughters, at Charleston, c. 1976. (collection of Tobit Roche)

24. Paul Roche with Duncan Grant, holding a copy of "Enigma Variations And," for which he designed the cover, see Number 97.

PLATE 6

25. Charleston, Firle, home of Duncan Grant.

26. Duncan Grant's bedroom at Charleston: the carpet in the foreground was designed by Douglas Davidson, the cover on the bench by the window was designed by Vanessa Bell and worked in cross stitch by Ethel Grant, and among the pictures on the walls, at the head on the bed, is Vanessa Bell's "Still Life with Beer Bottle," 1913.

PLATE 7

27. Duncan Grant's studio at Charleston. On the left can be seen one panel of the screen he designed for the opening of the Omega Workshops in 1913, on the right is a cabinet which once belonged to W. M. Thackeray. The fireplace was decorated by Duncan in 1928.

28. Duncan Grant painting in Vanessa Bell's bedroom, c. 1976, with his portraits of her sons Julian and Quentin and their daughter Angelica on the walls. Photo by Chris Ware.

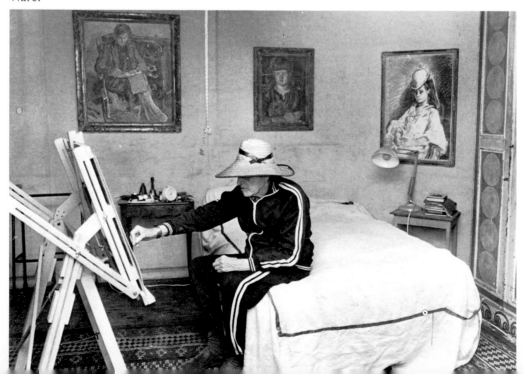

PLATE 8

29. War scene with elephants and monkeys, from a sketchbook from Duncan Grant's childhood. (collection of Paul Roche)

30. War scene with soldiers and naked men, from a later sketchbook from Duncan Grant's childhood. (collection of Paul Roche)

PLATE 9

31. Pencil sketch, Streatley-on-Thames, 1902. (collection of Paul Roche)

32. Nude study, 1902.   33. Nude study, 1902.

(collection of Paul Roche)   (collection of Paul Roche)

PLATE 10

34. "The Kitchen," 1902. (The Tate Gallery, London) Painted at Streatley-on-Thames, this is one of Grant's earliest surviving paintings. His life-long interest in patterns, in the figure, in still life, and in views seen from one room to another are all in evidence in this work. Compare with Number 35, painted twelve years later.

PLATE 11

35. "The Kitchen," begun 1914, reworked 1916-17. (Keynes' Collection, King's College, Cambridge) The woman on the far left is Vanessa Bell. The foreground figure is related to a Grant designed for a 1913 Omega Christmas card, and the naked boy is a portrait of one of Vanessa's sons, see Number 10.

PLATE 12

36. "Le Crime et le Châtiment," 1909. (The Tate Gallery, London) Marjorie
Strachey posed for this atmospheric portrait, in which she is overcome by the gloom of
Dostoevsky's novel. On the other side of the canvas is a portrait of her brother Lytton
Strachey, see Number 37.

37. "Lytton Strachey," 1909. (The Tate Gallery, London) Strachey fell in love with
Duncan Grant, his younger cousin, and for a time his affections were returned.

PLATE 13

38. "James Strachey," 1909-10. (The Tate Gallery, London) Rupert Brooke, James' schoolmate, called this "the famous picture of James' legs." Grant enjoyed painting into his pictures works by other artists. Note Japanese screen.

39. "Pamela," 1911. (Yale Center for British Art, Paul Mellon Fund) Roger Fry's daughter, by the lily pond at her father's house, Durbins.

PLATE 14

40. "Bathing," 1911. (The Tate Gallery, London) Done for the dining room of the Borough Polytechnic, with "Football," Number 41, these large murals gave Grant an opportunity to work on a large scale.

PLATE 15

41. "Football," 1911. (The Tate Gallery, London) These murals brought Grant his first public success. The Tate Gallery bought them in 1931.

Plate 16

42. "John Maynard Keynes," by Gwen Raverat. (The National Portrait Gallery, London) Keynes fell deeply in love with Grant, and remained a devoted friend all his life. He established an independent income for Grant in 1937.

43. "John Maynard Keynes," 1909. (Keynes' Collection, King's College, Cambridge) Keynes and Grant went for a two month holiday to the Orkney Islands, which the jealous Lytton Strachey called their "honeymoon." It was not just a romantic idyll, however. Both men continued their work, Grant sketching and painting, and Keynes (who was to become the most famous economist of the twentieth century) working on his theory of probability, as shown in this portrait.

PLATE 17

PLATE 18

44. "David Garnett," 1918. (collection of Mario Sartori) Duncan Grant's lover during the First World War, known as "Bunny."

PLATE 19

45. "David Garnett." (Thos. Agnew & Sons, London) Bunny Garnett was living at Charleston with Duncan Grant and Vanessa Bell when their daughter Angelica was born in 1918. Bunny prophesied that he would marry her when she grew up. They were married in 1942.

PLATE 20

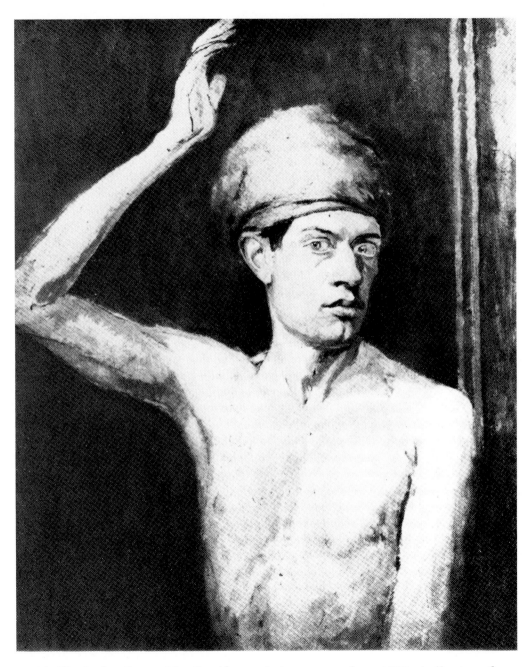

46. "Study for Composition," self-portrait in green turban, 1910. (collection of Marchioness of Dufferin and Ava) Grant originally painted himself wearing a tall headdress or holding a jar on his head, in the manner of the figures seen on the far right in Number 50 and in Number 60. He loved turbans; see Number 7 and Number 58.

PLATE 21

47. "The Bath." (collection of Paul Roche) Grant made several versions of this painting.

48. "Abstract Kinetic Collage Painting With Sound," 1914. (The Tate Gallery, London) This scroll-like work was nearly 15 feet long, and meant to be unfurled to music.

PLATE 22

49. Mural of tennis players, painted at 38 Brunswick Square, 1912. (The Tate Archive, London) Grant lived in this house with Maynard Keynes and later with Adrian Stephen.

PLATE 23

50. Murals commissioned by John Maynard Keynes for his rooms at Webb Court, King's College, 1910-11. (King's College, Cambridge) Grant was fascinated by the theme of a ring of dancers.

51. Murals for Keynes' rooms at Webb Court (King's College, Cambridge), executed 1919-20.

PLATE 24

52. "In Memoriam: Rupert Brooke," 1915. (Yale Center for British Art, Paul Mellon Fund) Grant's memorial for the poet Rupert Brooke and his brother Alfred, both victims of the First World War. The painting was important to the artist, who kept it in his studio where it remained unexhibited for sixty years.

PLATE 25

53. "Abstract Painting," 1978. (collection of the author: DBT.13) Shortly before his death at the age of 93, Grant was preoccupied with a series of abstract paintings, based on rectangles, which recall the "In Memorian: Rupert Brooke" of 63 years before.

PLATE 26

54. "Vanessa Bell," 1918. (National Portrait Gallery, London) Painted at the time of their love affair, Vanessa was pregnant with Duncan Grant's child.

PLATE 27

55. "Vanessa Bell," 1942. (The Tate Gallery, London)

PLATE 28

56. "The Pond at Charleston," 1959. (The Reader's Digest Association, Inc.)

PLATE 29

57. "The French Window, Charleston," 1953. (The Reader's Digest Association, Inc.)

PLATE 30

58. "Black and White Nudes, with Hats, Embracing."
(collection of the author: DBT.3)

59. "Two Nudes, Wrestling." (collection of the author: DBT.9)

PLATE 31

60. "Two Nudes on a Beach." (Yale Center for British Art, Gift of Joseph McCrindle)

PLATE 32

61. "Flowers and Leaves," 1936. (Victoria and Albert Museum. Circ. 89A-1937) Screen-printed on cotton velvet, this fabric was part of the commission from the Cunard White Star Steamship Company for their luxury liner the Queen Mary. All Grant's designs, textiles and paintings were rejected.

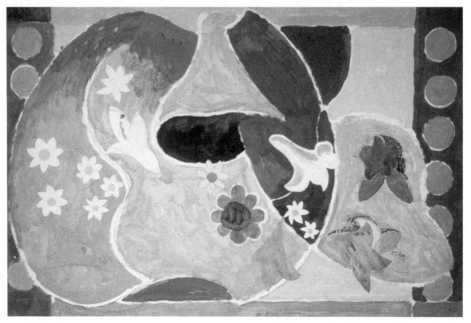

62. Design for a rug, c. 1936. (The Reader's Digest Association, Inc.) Some of Grant's favorite design motifs, as also seen in the fabric pattern, Number 61, were bell-like flowers, daisy-like flowers, leaf shapes and rows of circles or balls, see also Number 96.

PLATE 33

63. "Apollo and Daphne," 1932-33. (Victoria and Albert Museum. Circ. 335-1938) Manufactured by Allan Walton Textiles, the fabric was screen-printed on cotton and rayon. It won a Medal of Merit at the 1937 Paris International Exhibition.

PLATE 34

64. "At the Ballet," 1933. (The Reader's Digest Association, Inc.)

PLATE 35

65. "Lydia Lopokova," 1923. (Reproduced by permission of the Provost and Fellows of King's College, Cambridge [Keynes' Collection], on loan to the Fitzwilliam Museum) Maynard Keynes married the celebrated Russian ballerina Lydia Lopokova, and Grant designed sets and costumes for her.

PLATE 36

66. Vaslav Nijinksy, 1910, photo by Druet. (New York Public Library, Dance Collection) In costume for La Danse Siamoise, Nijinsky was photographed in the garden of the painter Jacques-Emile Blanche, Duncan Grant's first teacher in Paris. Grant was fascinated by the great dancer and kept this photo in his studio. He used it in his "Still Life with Nijinsky," 1972.

67. "Nijinsky as the Favorite Slave, from the ballet Schéhérazade." (collection of the author: DBT.10)

68. "Nijinsky in the ballet Narcisse." (collection of the author: DBT.11)

PLATE 37

69. "Pas de Deux." (collection of Paul Roche)

PLATE 38

70. "Barn at Charleston," c. 1940 (The Reader's Digest Association, Inc.)

71. "A Sussex Farm," 1936. (The Toledo Museum of Art)

PLATE 39

72. "Cornwall Houses." (The Durban Art Museum, South Africa)

73. "Harbor Scene." (collection of Paul Roche)

PLATE 40

74. "Dining Room Window," portrait of Duncan Grant and his daughter Angelica, 1940, by Vanessa Bell. (The Reader's Digest Association, Inc.) Not long before this picture was painted, Vanessa Bell had told Angelica that her father was not Clive Bell, as she had grown up believing, but Duncan Grant.

PLATE 41

75. "Artist's Studio at Charleston," 1967. (The Metropolitan Museum of Art, Gift of Arthur W. Cohen, 1985 [1985.36.2]) A portrait of Vanessa Bell, c.1955, in the collection of the Duke of Devonshire, shows her sitting in this chair. This picture was painted after her death. The designs on the walls were stencilled on by the two artists in 1945. The tiled table was made by Vanessa's son Quentin. At one time Matisse's "Le Port," left to her by Roger Fry, hung over the desk.

PLATE 42

76. "Man and Woman." (collection of the author: DBT.58)

77. "Man and Woman." (collection of the author: DBT.59)

PLATE 43

78. "Man, Woman and Child." (collection of Paul Roche)

PLATE 44

79. "Lismore Castle." (reproduced by permission of Her Grace the Duchess of Devonshire) Duncan Grant stayed on several occasions at Chatsworth, in Derbyshire, the home of the Duke and Duchess of Devonshire. He also visited Lismore Castle, their house in Ireland. This painting hangs in the bedroom of the Duchess, at Chatsworth.

PLATE 45

80. "The Duchess of Devonshire." (reproduced by permission of Her Grace the Duchess of Devonshire)

PLATE 46

81. "Black Nude." (collection of the author: DBT.26) This drawing was a study for
Number 82. The model was probably Patrick Nelson, who also modelled for Edward
le Bas.

PLATE 47

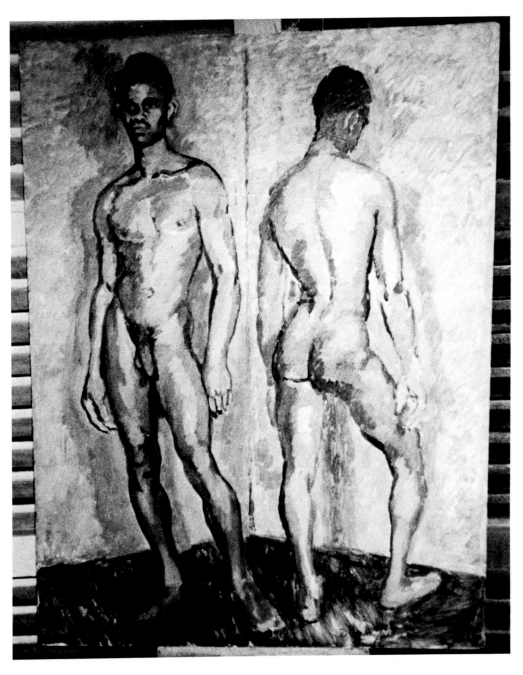

82. "Two Black Nudes." (collection of Paul Roche)

PLATE 48

83. "Paul Roche," 1946. (collection of Paul Roche)

PLATE 49

84. "Paul Roche," 1953. (collection of the author: DBT.28)

85. "Paul Roche on the rug at Bedford Square," 1946. This
is the first painting Duncan Grant did of Paul Roche.
(collection of Paul Roche)

PLATE 50

86. "Basketball Game," 1960. (collection of author: DBT.29)

PLATE 51

87. "Wrestlers." (collection of the author: DBT.22)

PLATE 52

88. "The Bathers." (National Gallery of Victoria, Melbourne, Felton Bequest 1948)

PLATE 53

89. "The Steam Bath." (collection of the author: DBT.21)

PLATE 54

90. "Europa and the Bull." (collection of the author: DBT.61) This was an illustration for a poem by W. R. Rodgers.

PLATE 55

91. Illustration for "The Rime of the Ancient Mariner." (Harry Ransom Humanities Research Center, University of Texas at Austin)

PLATE 56

92. Cover design for "Monkey" by Wu Ch'eng-en, translated by Arthur Waley. (Harry Ransom Humanities Research Center, University of Texas at Austin)

93. Screen. (collection of David Shapiro)

PLATE 57

94. Portrait of Paul Roche, 1966.
(collection of Paul Roche)

95. Cover design for "Water Colours and Drawings." (Harry Ransom Humanities Research Center, University of Texas at Austin)

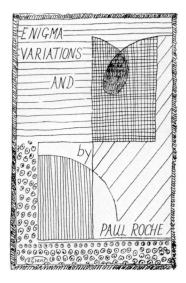

97. Cover design for "Enigma Variations And." (collection of the author)

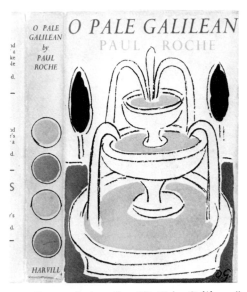

96. Cover design for "O Pale Galilean." (collection of Paul Roche) Grant did a painting using the same design.

PLATE 58

98. Self Portrait. (collection of Carolyn Heilbrun)

PLATE 59

99. "Violet Hammersley," 1954. (reproduced by permission of His Grace the Duke of Devonshire) Grant's fellow guests at Chatsworth sometimes included his old friend Violet Hammersley, and he painted her there. Compare this portrait with her photograph, Number 20. The present Duke of Devonshire has added many 20th century paintings, including work by Vanessa Bell, Augustus John, and Walter Sickert to the great collections of Old Masters at Chatsworth.

PLATE 60

100. "The Good Shepherd Ministers to His Flock," mock-up in the studio, with cut-out figures, for the mural for the Russell Chantry, dedicated to St. Blaise, in Lincoln Cathedral. Paul Roche was the model for the Christ.

101. On the far left can be seen a set-up for a still life, with a coffee pot and a spotted scarf, which was used in Number 102. (collection of Paul Roche)

PLATE 61

102. "Poppies," c.1955. (collection of Cordelia Roche)

PLATE 62

103. "Cheese Dish." (collection of Kevin Patterson)

PLATE 63

104. "Turkish Café," 1974 (collection of Pandora Smith)

PLATE 64

105. "Still Life with Matisse," 1971. (reproduced by permission of Her Majesty Queen Elizabeth the Queen Mother)